The California Privacy Rights Act (CPRA)

An implementation and compliance guide

The California Privacy Rights Act (CPRA)

An implementation and compliance guide

PRESTON BUKATY

IT Governance Publishing

Every possible effort has been made to ensure that the information contained in this book is accurate at the time of going to press, and the publisher and the author cannot accept responsibility for any errors or omissions, however caused. Any opinions expressed in this book are those of the author, not the publisher. Websites identified are for reference only, not endorsement, and any website visits are at the reader's own risk. No responsibility for loss or damage occasioned to any person acting, or refraining from action, as a result of the material in this publication can be accepted by the publisher or the author.

Apart from any fair dealing for the purposes of research or private study, or criticism or review, as permitted under the Copyright, Designs and Patents Act 1988, this publication may only be reproduced, stored, or transmitted, in any form, or by any means, with the prior permission in writing of the publisher or, in the case of reprographic reproduction, in accordance with the terms of licenses issued by the Copyright Licensing Agency. Inquiries concerning reproduction outside those terms should be sent to the publisher at the following address:

IT Governance Publishing Ltd
Unit 3, Clive Court
Bartholomew's Walk
Cambridgeshire Business Park
Ely, Cambridgeshire
CB7 4EA
United Kingdom
www.itgovernancepublishing.co.uk

Formerly published as *The California Consumer Privacy Act (CCPA) – An implementation guide* in the United Kingdom in 2019 by IT Governance Publishing.

First published in the United Kingdom in 2021 by IT Governance Publishing.

ISBN 978-1-78778-286-0

ABOUT THE AUTHOR

Preston Bukaty is an attorney and consultant. He specializes in data privacy governance, risk, and compliance (GRC) projects, from data inventory audits to gap analyses, contract management, and remediation planning. His compliance background and experience operationalizing compliance in a variety of industries give him a strong understanding of the legal issues presented by international regulatory frameworks. Having conducted more than 3,000 data mapping audits, he also understands the practical realities of project management in operationalizing compliance initiatives.

Preston's legal experience and enthusiasm for technology make him uniquely suited to understanding the business impact of privacy regulations such as the General Data Protection Regulation (GDPR) and the CPRA. He has advised more than 250 organizations engaged in businesses as varied as SaaS platforms, mobile geolocation applications, GNSS/telematics tools, financial institutions, fleet management software, architectural/engineering design systems, and web hosting. He also teaches certification courses on GDPR compliance and ISO 27001 implementation, and writes on data privacy law topics.

Preston lives in Denver, Colorado. Before working as a data privacy consultant, he worked for an international GPS software company, advising business areas on compliance issues across 140 countries. Preston holds a juris doctorate from the University of Kansas School of Law, along with a basketball signed by Hall of Fame coach Bill Self.

CONTENTS

Contents

INTRODUCTION

The lack of comprehensive privacy regulation in the US presents a unique set of compliance challenges for companies that collect personal data. Although a patchwork of sector-specific and state laws exist, they rarely deal with the pervasive collection and sale of people's personal information. Penalties for data breaches attempt to protect personal information by punishing companies for after-the-fact violations, but this does little to safeguard information in real time.

Ultimately, the issue is that data peddling is so pervasive. In the 2000s, Internet service companies such as Facebook and Google began collecting vast troves of personal data in an effort to personalize their online offerings. Search engines, for example, could consistently return better search results if user input and activity was analyzed. Social media networks, in contrast, tugged at innate human drives to connect and share with each other, which instilled a desire to maintain increasingly curated online profiles filled with personal details. Over time, these companies were able to monetize this information by using increasingly complex technologies that broadened the scale and complexity of data gathering to create detailed informational profiles on a person. Someone's interests, their income, political preference, or location – all could be used to tweak and sell ads targeted directly at that individual.

Marketers were willing to pay for access to this data, and so companies such as Facebook and Google profited immensely during the mid-to-late 2000s under a relative lack of regulatory oversight. Most consumers did not really grasp the technology behind this "surveillance capitalism," and often failed to realize just how vast the data collection network had grown. The technology companies were partly to blame – in amassing their fortune they employed a growing number of lobbyists at the state and federal levels to support their business model. So, for a long time, the issue went unresolved but not unnoticed.

In 2012, "a team of experts at Obama's Commerce Department worked on drafting a detailed privacy bill," but the proposal was "robbed [...] of both momentum and moral authority" by the revelations of Edward Snowden.[1] Snowden, "a former contractor for the National Security Agency, [...] revealed how the N.S.A. was collecting rivers of personal data – emails, photos, instant-message conversations – from nine leading internet companies, including Google, Facebook, Yahoo and Microsoft."[2]

Around this time, Alastair Mactaggart, a San Francisco-based real estate developer, began thinking about these rivers of personal data. He discovered that, "The rules [...] were largely established by the very companies that most relied on your data, in privacy policies and end-user agreements most people never actually read."[3]

---

[1] Nicholas Confessore, "The Unlikely Activists Who Took On Silicon Valley—and Won", August 2018, *www.nytimes.com/2018/08/14/magazine/facebook-google-privacy-data.html*.

[2] Ibid.

[3] Ibid.

In response, Mactaggart hired a team of consultants to help draft and propose a new privacy bill for California – something aimed directly at the surveillance capitalists, attempting to restore a semblance of balance between the tech titans, their customers (marketers), and their products (average people). What came about was a ballot initiative that expanded the definition of personal data, granted a set of rights to consumers (access, deletion, opt-out) akin to European legislation, and a private right of action that expanded enforcement powers to all end users.

The Consumer Right to Privacy Act of 2018

Mactaggart's original ballot initiative included several key provisions. Most notably, it broadened the definition of "personal information" to contemplate new technologies and cover a variety of increasingly complex (and profitable) data elements. It also included a private right of action that enabled the law to be enforced by actual consumers whose rights were violated (in addition to California's attorney general).

Naturally, tech companies were antithetical to any proposed legislation that would curtail the influx of income earned from the unregulated collection and sale of such information. Business advocates in California also feared the expanded enforcement rights, which created an unknown, potentially huge litigation liability. They feared the cost of fighting vast numbers of private actions would deter businesses from operating in California, or even increase the cost of services for consumers. Thus, the ballot initiative met with strong opposition from government and industry, and it seemed unlikely the measure would pass in its original form. That is, until the Cambridge Analytica scandal of 2018.

In March 2018, Facebook quietly announced "it was suspending a political analytics firm called Cambridge Analytica from its platform after it had 'received reports' that Cambridge had improperly obtained and held data about Facebook users."[4] What followed was an onslaught of investigative reporting that revealed "a contractor for Cambridge had harvested private information from more than 50 million Facebook users, exploiting the social-media activity of a huge swath of the American electorate and potentially violating United States election laws."[5] Public outrage ensued, and suddenly Mactaggart's proposal gained enough support to overwhelm government and industry opposition. It seemed that if companies were unable or unwilling to regulate their collection and use of personal information, the voters of California would force them to do so.

AB-375

In response, the California legislature rushed to draft something that would effectively enforce privacy rights and also protect the business interests of their multibillion-dollar constituents. AB-375 was signed on June 21, 2018, and California's governor signed on June 28. The new law

---

[4] Nicholas Confessore, "The Unlikely Activists Who Took On Silicon Valley—and Won", August 2018, *www.nytimes.com/2018/08/14/magazine/facebook-google-privacy-data.html*.

[5] Ibid.

expanded on some things previously unmentioned by Mactaggart's proposal, but it also changed some details.

For example, AB-375 required businesses to disclose categories and specific pieces of information collected about California consumers, as well as the business reason for collecting or selling that information, and the categories of third parties that receive it. It also prohibited the sale of personal information related to a consumer under the age of 16 without explicit (i.e. opt-in) consent.

Most notably, AB-375 removed the consumer enforcement mechanism by gutting the private right of action found in Mactaggart's proposal. The new law conferred exclusive enforcement authority to California's attorney general for most provisions.[6] Consumers were left with a limited right to enforce paltry statutory penalties (in addition to actual damages) in the event of a data breach – $100 to $750 for:

> Any consumer whose nonencrypted or nonredacted personal information ... is subject to an unauthorized access and exfiltration, theft, or disclosure as a result of the business' violation of the duty to implement and maintain reasonable security procedures and practices appropriate to the nature of the information to protect the personal information.[7]

Unfortunately, the enforcement mechanism was complex. Basically, a consumer was required to first provide 30 days' written notice to the business, identifying specific statutory

---

[6] AB-375 § 1798.150(c).

[7] AB-375 § 1798.150(a)(1).

violations.[8] If a business cured the violation within 30 days, "no action for individual statutory damages or class-wide statutory damages may be initiated against the business."[9] Only if the business continued to violate the statute, in breach of the express written statement provided, could the consumer initiate an action against the business for breach of that statement (along with any other privacy act violation).[10]

In addition, consumers were required to notify the attorney general within 30 days of an action being filed.[11] The attorney general was to then notify the consumer of an intent to bring enforcement action, or allow the 30 days to lapse and allow the consumer to proceed with the action.[12] Needless to say, AB-375 needed some clarification.

SB-1121

On August 31, 2018, the California State Legislature passed SB-1121, amending provisions of AB-375 to address inconsistencies and help implement a more comprehensive

---

[8] AB-375 § 1798.150(b).

[9] AB-375 § 1798.150(b)(1).

[10] Ibid.

[11] AB-375 § 1798.150(b)(2),(3).

[12] Ibid.

consumer privacy act.[13] Among other things, SB-1121, now codified as the "CCPA":

- Clarified what defines "personal information" to explain that the information must "identify, relate to, describe, or reasonably link, directly or indirectly, with a particular consumer or household"[14]
- Delayed attorney general enforcement until six months after publication of implementing regulations, or July 1, 2020, whichever comes first (the attorney general being responsible for drafting and adopting those implementing regulations)[15]
- Limited civil penalties to $2,500 for each violation, up to $7,500 for each intentional violation, and possible injunction for organizations that violate the law[16]
- Changed the private right of action to no longer require attorney general notification, but kept its scope limited to data breaches caused "as a result of the business's violation of the duty to implement and maintain

---

[13] *https://leginfo.legislature.ca.gov/faces/billTextClient.xhtml?bill_id=2 01720180SB1121*.

[14] SB 1121 § 1798.140(o)(1).

[15] SB 1121 § 1798.185(a),(c).

[16] Cal. Civ. Code § 1798.155(a).

reasonable security procedures and practices appropriate to the nature of the information"[17]

- Carved out exceptions for coverage under other, similar laws (e.g. the Health Insurance Portability and Accountability Act (HIPAA), or parts of the state's Constitution)[18]
- Required a business that collects personal information to disclose consumers' right to delete that information, with such notices to be provided in a reasonably accessible form (as opposed to the website or online privacy policy, which was originally the case)[19]

The CCPA came into effect on January 1, 2020, and enforcement began on January 1, 2020. The law still applies to organizations that do business in California (regardless of where they are based), and:

- Have a gross annual turnover of $25 million or more
- Buy, receive, sell, or share the personal data of 50,000 or more consumers, or
- Derive 50% or more of their annual revenue from selling consumers' data.

Organizations that fail to comply with the CCPA's requirements are subject to civil penalties of up to $7,500 and a civil suit that gives every affected consumer the right

---

[17] SB 1121 § 1798.150(a)(1).

[18] SB 1121 § 1798.145(c).

[19] SB 1121 § 1798.105(b).

to seek between $100 and $750 in damages per incident, or actual damages if higher.

Proposition 24

Unsatisfied with the evolution of legislation that led to the CCPA, Alastair Mactaggart founded "Californians for Consumer Privacy," an advocacy group intending to rewrite the law with stronger consumer protections and more sensible business requirements. Notably, California law allows for proposed initiatives to be placed on the ballot for public vote if they receive 675,000 valid signatures.

On May 4, 2020, Californians for Consumer Privacy announced that it had collected more than 900,000 signatures to qualify the CPRA (California Privacy Rights Act) for the November 2020 ballot. Also known as 'CCPA 2.0', the CPRA enhances privacy protections established by the CCPA and builds on consumer rights.

The measure was passed, with voter support about 56% of the electorate. Proposition 24, also known as the CPRA, effectively replaces the CCPA and bolsters privacy protections for California consumers. While many elements of the two laws are similar, there are some striking differences that could impact CCPA implementation plans:

- Limiting deletion rights that apply to unstructured data
- Exempting more small businesses by raising the threshold for what defines a 'business' processing personal information
- Extending current one-year exemptions for certain employee and business-to-business data

- Carving out a separate, sub-definition of 'sensitive data', akin to what is seen in the New York SHIELD Act; new, separate requirements would apply to this subset of data
- A new right to data minimization with retention requirements related to personal data
- A right to know, access, and receive personal information collected before the 12-month lookback period for data collected on or after January 1, 2022
- New definitions and obligations related to cross-context behavioral advertising
- Amending breach liability to include an email address in combination with a password or security question
- Establishing a new regulatory enforcement body: the California Privacy Protection Agency

As is likely clear, the legislative evolution of this proposal-turned-initiative-turned-law is complex, and requires careful reading to understand the actual requirements for organizations.

CHAPTER 1: CPRA JURISDICTION – TERRITORIAL

Relevant provisions of the California Civil Code that collectively make up the California Privacy Rights Act (CPRA) consistently refer to the rights of consumers as they apply to a "business." For example, "A consumer shall have the right to request that a business that collects a consumer's personal information disclose" certain things to that consumer.[20] Or, "A consumer shall have the right to request that a business delete any personal information about the consumer which the business has collected from the consumer."[21] As a result, the law's applicability hinges on key definitions of a "business," and, like all laws, organizations will need to carefully review definitions and terms to determine which portions of the statute apply.

Although many legal instruments include key terms as part of introductory text, the definitions for terms found in the CPRA are less obviously located. Many key terms can be found in section 1798.140. For example, "business" is defined in section 1798.140(d) as:

(1) A sole proprietorship, partnership, limited liability company, corporation, association, or other legal entity that is organized or operated for the profit or financial benefit of its shareholders or other owners, that collects consumers' personal information, or on the behalf of

---

[20] Cal. Civ. Code § 1798.110(a).

[21] Cal. Civ. Code § 1798.105(a).

which such information is collected and that alone, or jointly with others, determines the purposes and means of the processing of consumers' personal information, that does business in the State of California, and that satisfies one or more of the following thresholds:

(A) As of January 1 of the calendar year, had annual gross revenues in excess of twenty-five million dollars ($25,000,000) in the preceding calendar year, as adjusted pursuant to paragraph (5) of subdivision (a) of Section 1798.185.

(B) Alone or in combination, annually buys, sells, or shares the personal information of 100,000 or more consumers or households.

(C) Derives 50 percent or more of its annual revenues from selling, or sharing consumers' personal information.

(2) Any entity that controls or is controlled by a business, as defined in paragraph (1), and that shares common branding with the business and with whom the business shares consumers' personal information. "Control" or "controlled" means ownership of, or the power to vote, more than 50 percent of the outstanding shares of any class of voting security of a business; control in any manner over the election of a majority of the directors, or of individuals exercising similar functions; or the power to exercise a controlling influence over the management of a company. "Common branding" means a shared name, servicemark, or trademark.

This lengthy definition is not easy to understand. In order to know if the CPRA applies, an organization must first determine whether it does business in the State of California, such that the average consumer would understand that two or more entities are commonly owned.

Although the CPRA does not elaborate on what it specifically means to "do business in the State of California," there is relevant case law that can provide guidance. First, courts will look for general personal jurisdiction, which relates to a court's authority to hear cases within its established geographic area.

Typically, an incorporated business entity will be subject to the general personal jurisdiction of its home state. This is generally considered the state of incorporation, and/or the place of principal business (i.e. its headquarters).[22] For many organizations, this will mean that they can be subject to the general jurisdiction of two states. For example, if a company is incorporated in Delaware and its headquarters is in California, both Delaware and California will have general jurisdiction over the company. Thus, any organization actually established in California – perhaps by virtue of registering with the Secretary of State, among other things – should consider itself subject to the general jurisdiction of California's courts. Also, if the organization maintains a physical presence in California, the law will most likely apply.

However, there remains a question of extraterritorial reach. The issue is whether California, as a sovereign state, can apply its laws and regulations to organizations based outside

---

[22] US Supreme Court, *Daimler AG v. Bauman et al.,* 571 U.S.___ (2014). *www.supremecourt.gov/opinions/13pdf/11-965_1qm2.pdf.*

the state but operating within it. These situations are often complex, and critical distinctions in a case can rely on individual factual circumstances. What if a business is not operating within the physical confines of the state but maintains a limited amount of business connections with California consumers? Does this subject the actions of an organization based in one state to the sovereignty of another state's courts? If one organization can therefore be held accountable by multiple (possibly many) states all at once, how many business connections with a state are necessary for that state to establish jurisdiction? In particular, how many connections with California consumers are necessary for a California law to apply to an organization based in another state?

When US courts fail to establish general jurisdiction, they then look to specific jurisdiction. Specific jurisdiction relates to the amount of contacts that a defendant has with a state. The idea is that a court operating in one state may not have sufficient authority over an out-of-state defendant to claim general jurisdiction by virtue of geography, but, based on the actions of the defendant – either by working within the state or dealing with local residents – a sufficient level of contact is established to grant the local court jurisdiction over the out-of-state defendant.

Typically, the defendant must have "purposefully avail[ed] itself of the privilege of conducting activities within the forum State," or have purposefully directed its conduct into the court's state.[23] For example, if a defendant commits a crime in one particular state, that state court will have specific jurisdiction as it relates to the crime, regardless of where the defendant organization is based. Keep in mind that the organization will also be subject to the jurisdiction of the state where it is based, so in theory there is always at least one court to enforce rulings. The question, as mentioned earlier, ultimately relates to extraterritorial reach and the sovereignty of state laws under the US Constitution. It also relates to fairness. Defendants should not have the burden of having to appear in multiple state courts if the matter really does not relate to that state. Moreover, plaintiffs should not be able to sue defendants in multiple states if there is no basis (or need) for that court to enforce additional judgment.

Again, these situations are sometimes complex, and increasingly so in the modern business environment. Large organizations may operate across the country, and thus maintain contact with every state all at once. Because they operate at a national level, it may be difficult to determine which states may exercise jurisdiction over an action that was purposely directed at all states, but not any one in particular.

Consider a company that markets and sells products nationally, such as a customer relationship management (CRM) software vendor. Should that company be subject to the jurisdiction of all state courts (and thus possibly have to appear in all state courts) simply because a few people in

---

[23] *J. McIntyre Machinery, Ltd. v. Nicastro*, 564 U.S. 873, 877 (2011) (plurality opinion) (quoting *Hanson v. Denckla*, 357 U.S. 235, 253 (1958)).

each state bought the allegedly liable product? Probably not, as it would place an unfair burden on the defendant, in addition to constitutional questions of state power. This issue also becomes especially important in the context of class-action lawsuits, where huge groups of plaintiffs can be built up across the country. Therefore, in order to establish specific jurisdiction, a court must consider whether the actions of the defendant establish a sufficient level of contact with that state.

So, what is a sufficient level of contact? The California Supreme Court attempted to answer this question in 2016. In *Bristol-Myers Squibb Co. v. Superior Court (Anderson)*, a group of plaintiffs, comprising mainly non-California residents, sued the pharmaceutical company Bristol-Myers Squibb Company (BMS) over alleged health defects caused by its product Plavix.[24] The issue was that these plaintiffs sued BMS in California for liabilities under California law, despite there being no real connection to California. "The nonresident plaintiffs did not allege that they obtained Plavix through California physicians or from any other California source; nor did they claim that they were injured by Plavix or were treated for their injuries in California."[25] So, was a California court capable of enforcing judgment on an organization (in addition to the court where the organization was based) over actions that did not take place in California? And perhaps more importantly, could a group of plaintiffs – most with no real connection to California – sue a company

---

[24] *Bristol-Myers Squibb Co. v. Superior Court*, 377 P.3d 874 (Cal. 2016).

[25] *Bristol-Myers Squibb Co. v. Superior Court*, 582 U.S. ___, 2 (2017); citing 1 Cal. 5th 783, 790, 377 P.3d 874, 879 (2016).

in California courts for actions that did not take place in California?

In answering these questions, the California Supreme Court applied a "sliding scale approach to specific jurisdiction."[26] With this approach, the defendant's range of contacts can be used to show the connection between the defendant and the state.[27] As a result, the majority determined that it could exercise specific jurisdiction over the plaintiffs' claims "based on a less direct connection between BMS's [activities in California] and plaintiffs' claims than might otherwise be required [due to] BMS's extensive contacts with California."[28] Similarities between claims of the group's California and non-California residents effectively allowed California to hear the claims of the whole group.[29]

As mentioned earlier, the implications of these sorts of interpretations become immensely important when considering class-action lawsuits. The Court's ruling in *Bristol-Myers Squibb* would potentially allow class-action plaintiffs to sue defendants in California courts for violations of California law, even though the violations did not occur in California.

Such an important and far-reaching decision did not go without notice, and later in 2016 the United States Supreme Court granted a petition for a writ of certiorari (i.e. judicial

---

[26] 1 Cal. 5th, at 806, 377 P.3d, at 889.

[27] 1 Cal. 5th, at 806, 377 P.3d, at 889.

[28] Ibid.

[29] Id., at 803–806, 377 P.3d, at 887–889.

review) over the case. There, the Court described the "danger of the California approach"[30]:

> The mere fact that other plaintiffs were prescribed, obtained, and ingested Plavix in California—and allegedly sustained the same injuries as did the non-residents—does not allow the State to assert specific jurisdiction over the nonresidents' claims. As we have explained, "a defendant's relationship with a . . . third party, standing alone, is an insufficient basis for jurisdiction." *Walden*, 571 U. S., at ___ (slip op., at 8). This remains true even when third parties (here, the plaintiffs who reside in California) can bring claims similar to those brought by the nonresidents.

The Court explicitly noted that there must be "a connection between the forum and the specific claims at issue."[31] In this case, the relevant plaintiffs were non-California residents: "all the conduct giving rise to the nonresidents' claims occurred elsewhere," and the plaintiffs did not "claim to have suffered harm in that State. [...] It follows that the California courts cannot claim specific jurisdiction."[32]

So, it may be interpreted that California laws will apply to an organization established outside the state based on specific

---

[30] *Bristol-Myers Squibb Co. v. Superior Court of California*, 582 U.S. ___, 8 (2017).

[31] *Bristol-Myers Squibb Co. v. Superior Court of California*, 582 U.S. ___, 8 (2017).

[32] *Bristol-Myers Squibb Co. v. Superior Court of California*, 582 U.S. ___, 9 (2017).

personal jurisdiction if the plaintiffs at issue are California residents who claim to have suffered harm in the state. That is, if the claims at issue arise from the defendant's activities in the state. Of course, the laws will also apply if the organization is established in California (i.e. general jurisdiction by virtue of physical presence). Therefore, whether a business is "doing business in the state of California" – and therefore whether the CPRA applies to an organization – hinges on whether the organization maintains a physical presence in the state, or the degree to which California residents suffer harm in the state.

It should be noted that the CPRA does not prevent an organization from collecting or sharing a consumer's personal information "if every aspect of that commercial conduct takes place wholly outside of California."[33] This requires that:

- The business collected that information while the consumer was outside of California
- No part of the sale of the consumer's personal information occurred in California; and
- No personal information collected while the consumer was in California is sold.[34]

So, according to section 145, the CPRA does not apply to commercial conduct that takes place outside of California. That said, it is permissible for an organization to store personal information about a consumer while that person is

---

[33] Cal. Civ. Code § 1798.145 (a)(7).

[34] Ibid.

in California (e.g. on a device), and then collect that personal information when the consumer and the stored personal information leave.[35]

---

[35] Cal. Civ. Code § 1798.145 (a)(7).

CHAPTER 2: CPRA JURISDICTION – MATERIAL

As noted previously, the CPRA applies to a "business." Here, legislative guidance is a bit more direct. A "business" for the purposes of the CPRA is defined in section 1798.140(d)(1) as:

1. A sole proprietorship, partnership, limited liability company, corporation, association, or other legal entity
2. That is organized or operated for the profit or financial benefit of its shareholders or other owners
3. That collects consumers' personal information, or on the behalf of which such information is collected and that alone, or jointly with others, determines the purposes and means of the processing of consumers' personal information
4. That does business in the State of California.

Although this definition may seem obvious, there are some things to consider. First, the law only applies to an organization operated for "the profit or financial benefit" of its owners. Therefore, in its current state, the law does not apply to nonprofit organizations.

Second, the law only applies to organizations that collect personal information, or those that determine the purposes and means of processing that information. Great attention will likely be paid to this provision, as the rights of consumers – and thus, the responsibility of an organization to comply – apply to organizations that either collect information or determine the purposes of processing. For third-party service providers that generally only process a subset of data for limited purposes (and often based on explicit instructions), service agreements, data processing agreements, or other contractual arrangements will be critical. Exactly which organization determines the purposes and means of processing personal information will be the organization directly responsible for compliance with the CPRA; others in the data supply chain will likely only be liable for their limited processing.

This framework is similar to the one established by Europe's General Data Protection Regulation (GDPR). There, a "controller" is defined as the organization that "determines the purposes and means of the processing of personal data."[36] The data controller is responsible for demonstrating compliance with the GDPR under Article 24. In contrast, the data processor, which "processes personal data on behalf of the controller," is generally only responsible for assisting the controller in its compliance obligations.[37] Consequently, the data controller is responsible for managing data subject rights and responding to requests for information. The data processor, in turn, helps the controller facilitate those rights and responds to those requests based on how it processes data for the controller.

Lastly, the CPRA only applies to organizations that do business in the State of California. As explained in the previous section, an organization does business in the state if it is physically established there, or if its activities in the state

---

[36] GDPR, Article 4(7).

[37] GDPR, Article 28.

cause such harm to California residents that a California court could fairly adjudicate their claims.

That said, the CPRA's material jurisdiction also involves a threshold analysis. Naturally, not all laws apply to all people, and the same can be true for organizations. The CPRA only applies to organizations that:

1. Have gross revenues in excess of twenty-five million dollars ($25,000,000) in the preceding calendar year; or
2. Annually buy, receive, sell, or share the personal information of 100,000 or more consumers or households; or
3. Derive 50 percent or more of its annual revenues from selling or sharing consumers' personal information.[38]

Again, it is clear that the CPRA only applies to organizations engaged in a commercial enterprise. They must operate for a profit at minimum and, unless it is a large organization, they must profit from the sale or sharing of data in some way.

Now, the question of subsidiaries and other controlled entities may naturally arise. Section 1798.140(d)(2) explains that the law applies to "Any entity that controls or is controlled by a business, (defined above) and that shares common branding with the business and with whom the business shares consumers' personal information."[39] "Control" or "controlled" means ownership of, or voting power over, more than 50 percent of the outstanding shares of any class of voting security; control in any manner over

---

[38] Cal. Civ. Code § 1798.140(d)(1).

[39] Cal. Civ. Code § 1798.140(d)(2).

the election of a majority of the directors or individuals exercising similar functions; or the power to exercise a controlling influence over the management of a company.[40] The question remains as to what degree of control is required to meet the definition of "control" here as it applies to the influence of company management or the election of a board majority. The more sway or command that an organization has, though, over management of its subsidiary company or election of its board, the more likely it will be found that if the organization must comply, the subsidiary must comply as well (regardless of whether, for example, the subsidiary has no connection to California).

Of course, the law will not apply to organizations already covered under existing similar requirements. For example, organizations that collect or process protected health information governed by the "privacy, security, and breach notification rules [...] established pursuant to the Health Insurance Portability and Accountability Act of 1996 [HIPAA] and the Health Information Technology for Economic and Clinical Health Act [HITECH]."[41] It also does not apply to a consumer reporting agency's collecting or processing of personal information bearing on a consumer's credit worthiness (those organizations are covered by other laws).[42]

One final consideration: The law applies to organizations that collect personal information, or those that determine the

---

[40] Cal. Civ. Code § 1798.140(d)(2).

[41] Cal. Civ. Code § 1798.145(c)(1).

[42] Cal. Civ. Code § 1798.145(d)(1).

means and purposes of processing personal information. "Processing" is defined as "any operation or set of operations that are performed on personal information or on sets of personal information, whether or not by automated means."[43] Accordingly, as the definition of "processing" is broad enough to literally include "any operation [...] performed on personal information," it should be noted that almost any activity that occurs with regard to personal data will likely fall under the definition of "processing," and thus subject an organization to compliance with the CPRA. This can include passive activities, including storage of data.

---

[43] Cal. Civ. Code § 1798.140(y).

CHAPTER 3: THE CPRA – KEY DEFINITIONS

As noted earlier, many of the key definitions of terms and phrases are found in section 1798.140 of the CPRA. Much like the definition of "business," the terms defined in section 140 may have novel interpretations requiring careful analysis to understand how they apply to organizations.

Personal information

To start, it should be noted that the CPRA's definition of covered "personal information" encompasses a wide range of technological data markers. The term includes information "that identifies, relates to, describes, is reasonably capable of being associated with, or could reasonably be linked, directly or indirectly, with a particular consumer or household."[44] The statute then provides a non-exhaustive list of examples, but there are a few important things to consider at the outset.

First, note what could possibly be considered "personal information" by virtue of the definition's construction. According to the statute, "'Personal information' means information"[45] – there are no qualifiers preceding the word "information," so the *types* of information are not necessarily limited to any particular format, such as electronic data or paper files. All types of information are involved.

---

[44] Cal. Civ. Code § 1798.140(v)(1).

[45] Ibid.

The definition continues: "'Personal information' means information that identifies, relates to, describes, is reasonably capable of being associated with, or could reasonably be linked, directly or indirectly, with a particular consumer or household."[46] This is incredibly broad.

This definition includes not only descriptive information that directly identifies a person but also information that indirectly identifies them. This approach is also seen in Europe, where the GDPR defines personal data as any information that can directly or indirectly identify a natural person.[47] The idea is that some data on its own presents relatively little privacy risk to an individual, perhaps because the individual can only be truly identified based on substantial efforts to collect and combine the indirect information into something more cohesive. Consider the anonymized GPS coordinates of exercise fanatics who favor a certain smartwatch application. On its own, one set of anonymized GPS coordinates would do little to identify an individual user, let alone present a privacy risk.

However, this does not negate the inherent value of those indirect identifiers. As is often the case with technology, anything can be achieved with enough information. By collecting enough of those GPS datasets over time, one could effectively map the location and coordinates of all users. With relatively little additional information – for example, a known location or timestamped activity – one can quite easily pinpoint precisely which user was exercising where, and when. It is not difficult to imagine scenarios in which

---

[46] Cal. Civ. Code § 1798.140(v)(1).

[47] GDPR, Article 4(1).

individual users are directly identified by combining multiple indirect identifiers. Therefore, although indirect identifiers may offer little substantive value on their own, they can still present a risk to privacy in the aggregate.

Although the CPRA's use of direct and indirect identifiers mirrors the definition of personal data under the EU's GDPR, the CPRA goes further. Whereas the GDPR deals with information that "identifies" a person, the CPRA adds that personal information can include information that "…is reasonably capable of being associated with, or could reasonably be linked" to a person.[48] How exactly this piece of the definition will be interpreted and applied remains to be seen, but it certainly pulls a much larger subset of data into the covered definition of "personal information." For example, what level of indirect data linkage is necessary for that data to be considered "personal information"? When does an indirect link to data become so indirect that the "personal" aspect is essentially lost? Again, much of this remains to be seen, and will likely be sorted out through various interpretations of case law at the state level.

The CPRA does not stop there, however. The definition of "personal information" ends with the following phrase: "with a particular consumer or household."[49] What this means is that, unlike the GDPR, the CPRA does not apply solely to natural persons (wherever located). The CPRA applies to information – *any* information that relates to,

---

[48] Cal. Civ. Code § 1798.140(v)(1).

[49] Ibid.

describes, identifies, is reasonably linked to or associated with – a consumer *or* household.

"Household" is now defined under the CPRA (it was not under the CCPA). It means a group (however identified) of consumers who cohabitate with one another at the same residential address and share use of common device(s) or service(s).[50]

The CPRA also includes a non-exhaustive list of personal data elements that help outline the scope of coverage. To be clear, personal information *can include*, but is not limited to, the following types of data elements[51]:

- Identifiers such as a real name, alias, postal address, unique personal identifier, online identifier, Internet Protocol address, email address, account name, Social Security number, driver's license number, passport number, or other similar identifiers
- Any personal information described in subdivision (e) of Section 1798.80 (which relates to customer records)
- Characteristics of protected classifications under California or federal law
- Commercial information, including records of personal property, products or services purchased, obtained, or considered, or other purchasing or consuming histories or tendencies
- Biometric information

---

[50] Cal. Civ. Code § 1798.140(q).

[51] Cal. Civ. Code § 1798.140(v)(1)(A)–(L).

- Internet or other electronic network activity information, including, but not limited to, browsing history, search history, and information regarding a consumer's interaction with an Internet website, application, or advertisement
- Geolocation data
- Audio, electronic, visual, thermal, olfactory, or similar information
- Professional or employment-related information
- Non-public education information
- Inferences drawn from any of the information identified to create a profile about a consumer reflecting the consumer's preferences, characteristics, psychological trends, predispositions, behavior, attitudes, intelligence, abilities, and aptitudes
- "Sensitive personal information," which can include government ID numbers, account credentials or access information, precise geolocation, race, religion, ethnicity, sexual orientation, union membership, communication content, health data genetic data, and biometric information used for verification and identity purposes

Some key elements worthy of consideration:

- IP addresses are specifically enumerated.
- Biometric information, called out in subsection (E), is defined elsewhere as:

an individual's physiological, biological or behavioral characteristics, including information pertaining to an individual's deoxyribonucleic acid (DNA), that is used or intended to be used, singly or in combination with each other or with other identifying data, to establish individual identity. Biometric information includes, but is not limited to, imagery of the iris, retina, fingerprint, face, hand, palm, vein patterns, and voice recordings, from which an identifier template, such as a faceprint, a minutiae template, or a voiceprint, can be extracted, and keystroke patterns or rhythms, gait patterns or rhythms, and sleep, health, or exercise data that contain identifying information.[52]

- Browsing history, search history, and other information regarding a consumer's interaction with a website are also considered.

- Geolocation data is covered.

- Audio information (i.e. recorded calls and voice prompts) are covered, as is "visual, thermal, olfactory, or similar information." So, perhaps smells are included as "personal information"?

- "Inferences drawn from any of the information [...] to create a profile about a consumer reflecting the consumer's preferences, characteristics, psychological trends, predispositions, behavior, attitudes, intelligence, abilities, and aptitudes." This one is particularly interesting, because often those inferences drawn from

---

[52] Cal. Civ. Code 1798.140(c).

personal data to help create behavioral profiles of customer preference trends are formed based on intellectual property and other business trade secrets. The question remains as to whether covered entities will be required to simply provide the customer profile and treat that as "personal information," or also provide insight into the algorithms and mechanisms that create those profiles.

Importantly, covered "personal information" does not include publicly available information or "lawfully obtained, truthful information that is a matter of public concern." As a result, information that has already been manifestly made public may not fall within the scope of the CPRA. The idea is that the information is already public, so why work further to protect the privacy of public information? That said, it should be noted that the law states that "'Publicly available' does not mean biometric information collected by a business about a consumer without the consumer's knowledge."[53] For this reason, it can likely be assumed that in order for information to qualify as "public," and therefore not be subject to the provisions of the CPRA, that information must have been made public with the knowledge of the consumer.

Aggregate consumer information

Other definitions found in section 1798.140 are equally important when understanding the interplay between various sections of the CPRA and its overall applicability. Consider the definition of "aggregate consumer information":

---

[53] Cal. Civ. Code § 1798.140(v)(2).

information that relates to a group or category of consumers, from which individual consumer identities have been removed, that is not linked or reasonably linkable to any consumer or household, including via a device.[54]

The definition goes on to explain that "'Aggregate consumer information' does not mean one or more individual consumer records that have been deidentified."

Two things are important with regard to this particular definition. First, it is vital for an organization to understand what constitutes "aggregate consumer information," because that dictates overall applicability of the law. Elsewhere in the legislation, section 145 of the Act makes clear that "The obligations imposed on businesses by this title shall not restrict a business's ability" to do certain things, including common sense obligations such as complying with other laws or cooperating with law enforcement agencies.[55] It also does not prevent an organization from collecting, selling, or sharing a consumer's personal information "if every aspect of that commercial conduct takes place wholly outside of California."[56]

Yet the section explains one final set of activities that the CPRA cannot restrict: the collection, use, retention, storage, or disclosure of consumer information that is either

---

[54] Cal. Civ. Code § 1798.140(b).

[55] Cal. Civ. Code § 1798.145(a)(1)–(4).

[56] Cal. Civ. Code § 1798.145(a)(7).

deidentified or in the aggregate.[57] So, the definition of "aggregate consumer information" is paramount. For example, large-scale marketing analytics, which typically provide substantial business value and are often sold at a corresponding price, may constitute "aggregate consumer information" and thus not be subject to the requirements of the CPRA.

Essentially, aggregate information is information about a group, with individual consumer identities removed. As a result, the information is not linked or linkable to any one particular consumer (or household). Rather, the information should be linked/linkable to the group at large – more akin to a single, conglomerate mass of anonymous individuals.

Pseudonymization and deidentification

Interestingly, "anonymous" and "anonymize" are not defined in the CPRA. However, "pseudonymize" is, and it is markedly different from the definition of deidentified data. Remember, the CPRA does not restrict the collection, use, retention, storage, or disclosure of consumer information that is either deidentified or in the aggregate.[58]

"Deidentified" is defined as information that cannot "reasonably be used to infer information about, or otherwise be linked to, a particular consumer."[59] In addition, the organization must take reasonable measures to ensure that the information cannot be associated with a consumer or

---

[57] Cal. Civ. Code § 1798.145(a)(6).

[58] Cal. Civ. Code § 1798.145(a)(6).

[59] Cal. Civ. Code § 1798.140(m).

household, while also making no further attempt on its own to reidentify the information; any recipients of the information must be contractually obligated to these same requirements.[60]

In contrast, "pseudonymize" is defined as a process that "renders the personal information no longer attributable to a specific consumer without the use of additional information."[61] The difference is that deidentified data cannot be linked to a particular consumer – it is incapable of even being associated with that consumer – whereas pseudonymized data is no longer attributable without additional information. It can be reidentified, whereas deidentified data has been totally stripped of its identifying characteristics.

Granted, the process of pseudonymization, or separating information from its personal attributes, requires some additional steps, much like deidentification. Here, the organization is required to keep this additional attributing information separate from the pseudonymized set, and the additional information must be subject to both technical and organizational measures that ensure attribution (i.e. identification) does not take place.[62]

Pseudonymized data might look something like this:

---

[60] Cal. Civ. Code § 1798.140(m).

[61] Cal. Civ. Code § 1798.140(aa).

[62] Ibid.

Table 1: Pseudonymized Data

Customer	Expenses Q1	Expenses Q2	Expenses Q3	Expenses Q4
A	$348	$297	$190	$410
B	$72	$89	$90	$101
C	$149	$120	$133	$122
D	$301	$411	$295	$400

In this instance, there would be a separate dataset held elsewhere with identifying information linked to the customer alias, such as the customer's name, address, and billing information. Because the preceding data cannot be linked to a specific consumer or household without that additional information, the data is successfully pseudonymized. Deidentified data, however, would have no access to data that would identify the customers.

Collects, collected, collection

"Collects," "collected," or "collection" refer to the "buying, renting, gathering, obtaining, receiving, or accessing any personal information pertaining to a consumer <u>by any means</u>" (emphasis added).[63] This includes "receiving

---

[63] Cal. Civ. Code § 1798.140(f).

information from the consumer, either actively or passively, or by observing the consumer's behavior."[64]

Consumer

"Consumer" means a natural person who is a California resident.[65] "Resident" is defined in the California Code of Regulations as every individual in the state for "other than a temporary or transitory purpose," and those who are domiciled in the state who may only leave for a temporary purpose.[66] "Natural persons" also typically refers to a human being, as opposed to a "legal person" (e.g. LLC entity).

Device

Many provisions of the statute deal with the collection or processing of data via a "device" of some kind. This is generally defined as "any physical object that is capable of connecting to the Internet, directly or indirectly, or to another device."[67]

Homepage

"Homepage" means the introductory page of an Internet website and any Internet web page where personal information is collected."[68] This definition will become

---

[64] Cal. Civ. Code § 1798.140(f).

[65] Cal. Civ. Code § 1798.140(i).

[66] 18 CCR § 17014 (2017).

[67] Cal. Civ. Code § 1798.140(o).

[68] Cal. Civ. Code § 1798.140(p).

important when discussing the rights of consumers, and how to facilitate those rights.

Person

"Person" means an individual, proprietorship, firm, partnership, joint venture, syndicate, business trust, company, corporation, limited liability company, association, committee, and any other organization or group of persons acting in concert."[69] Note that rights in relation to data apply to consumers, not to persons. A "person" under the CPRA is not the equivalent of a "data subject" under the GDPR.

Research

Research with personal information collected during the course of a consumer's interactions with a business or device is subject to certain requirements.[70] Generally, though, "research" is understood in the context of academic research, and not merely internal research and development devoted to new products or increasing customer engagement. "Research," as defined here, "means scientific analysis, systematic study and observation, including [...] research that is designed to develop or contribute to public or scientific knowledge and that adheres [...] to all other applicable ethics and privacy laws, including but not limited

---

[69] Cal. Civ. Code § 1798.140(u).

[70] Cal. Civ. Code § 1798.140(ab).

to studies conducted in the public interest in the area of public health."[71]

Sell, selling, sale, sold

This is defined as the dissemination, disclosure, release, transfer, or other communication (oral or in writing), of a consumer's personal information for money or other valuable consideration.[72] Conversely, a business does not sell personal information when[73]:

- A consumer directs the business to intentionally disclose personal information, or intentionally interact with a third party
- The business uses or shares a consumer identifier to alert third parties that the consumer has opted out of the sale of their personal information, or limited the use of the consumer's sensitive personal information
- The business transfers the information as part of a merger, acquisition, bankruptcy, or other transaction, as long as the processing of the information continues in a manner consistent with descriptions of processing given to the consumer when the personal information was originally collected

---

[71] Cal. Civ. Code § 1798.140(ab).

[72] Cal. Civ. Code § 1798.140(ad)(1).

[73] Cal. Civ. Code § 1798.140(ad)(2)(A)–(C).

Third party

"Third party" means a person who is not one of the following:

- A business that collects personal information from consumers as a part of their interactions[74]
- A service provider to the business[75]
- A contractor[76]

Unique personal identifier

"Unique personal identifiers" are listed as a category of "identifiers" in the definition of covered "personal information."[77] "Unique personal identifiers" are defined as "a persistent identifier that can be used to recognize a consumer, a family, or a device that is linked to a consumer or family, over time and across different services."[78] Much like the definition of "personal information," the definition of "unique personal identifier" includes a non-exhaustive list of examples, including:

- A device identifier
- An Internet Protocol (IP) address

---

[74] Cal. Civ. Code § 1798.140(ai)(1).

[75] Cal. Civ. Code § 1798.140(ai)(2).

[76] Cal. Civ. Code § 1798.140(ai)(3).

[77] Cal. Civ. Code § 1798.140(v)(1)(A).

[78] Cal. Civ. Code § 1798.140(aj).

- Cookies, beacons, pixel tags, mobile ad identifiers, or similar technology
- Customer number, unique pseudonym, or user alias
- Telephone numbers
- Or other forms of persistent or probabilistic identifiers that can be used to identify a particular consumer or device that is linked to a consumer or family

Now, some things to consider. First, as noted elsewhere, the amount of information covered by the CPRA's definition of "personal information" explicitly includes a wide range of technological markers. In contrast, Europe's GDPR points out in Recital 30 that "online identifiers provided by their devices, applications, tools and protocols [...] may leave traces" which, when combined, can be used to create profiles that identify someone.[79] However, recitals of the GDPR are only meant to provide additional guidance, and they do not serve as actual statute. As a result, nowhere in the actual blackletter law of the GDPR is mention made of things such as IP addresses or mobile ad identifiers. "Personal data" is merely defined as information relating to a data subject. Yet, some EU courts have interpreted that IP addresses constitute personal data.

The CPRA starts with a similarly broad definition of "personal information" – remember, the term includes information "that identifies, relates to, describes, is reasonably capable of being associated with, or could reasonably be linked, directly or indirectly, with a particular

---

[79] GDPR, Recital 30.

consumer or household."[80] Nevertheless, the list of enumerated examples provides a level of guidance directly iterated in statute. Unlike the GDPR's recitals, the CPRA explicitly provides a list of example technologies that constitute "unique personal identifiers," and thus covers "personal information," to help direct public thinking on this topic. A large range of data markers are specifically spelled out to ensure creative legal departments do not define terms narrowly enough to avoid jurisdiction. Regardless of how IP addresses or mobile ad identifiers are interpreted as "personal data" under the GDPR, it is clear that this information, and more, is covered by the CPRA.

Second, the CPRA includes "other forms of persistent or probabilistic identifiers that can be used to identify a particular consumer or device."[81] "'Probabilistic identifier' means the identification of a consumer or a consumer's device to a degree of certainty [...] based on any categories of personal information included in, or similar to, the categories enumerated in the definition of personal information."[82] Under this definition, it could be argued that potentially any data marker that helps identify a consumer to a reasonable degree of certainty is considered a "probabilistic identifier," which constitutes a "unique personal identifier," which constitutes covered "personal information."

---

[80] Cal. Civ. Code § 1798.140(v)(1).

[81] Cal. Civ. Code § 1798.140(aj).

[82] Cal. Civ. Code § 1798.140(x).

Verifiable consumer request

This definition is critical because an organization is generally only obliged to respond to a consumer (i.e. give effect to their rights) "upon receipt of a verifiable consumer request."[83] So, in order to understand when an organization must reply to consumer requests – and thus how the organization should build its respective response processes – it must first understand what constitutes a consumer request.

First, a "verifiable consumer request" must be made by a consumer, by a consumer on behalf of their minor child, or by a person registered with the Secretary of State (i.e. a business) authorized by the consumer to act on their behalf, or by a person who has power of attorney or is acting as a conservator for the consumer.[84] At the same time, an organization is "not obligated to provide information to the consumer […] if the business cannot verify […] that the consumer making the request is the consumer about whom the business has collected information."[85]

The definition also refers to verification mechanisms made pursuant to paragraph (7) of subdivision (a) of Section 1798.185. This section basically explains that the attorney general will solicit public commentary on parts of the regulation, and in turn adopt further regulations to provide clarity on enforcement. Paragraph (7) specifically states that the attorney general will establish:

---

[83] Cal. Civ. Code § 1798.140(ak).

[84] Ibid.

[85] Ibid.

rules and procedures [...] to govern a business's determination that a request for information received from a consumer is a verifiable consumer request, including treating a request submitted through a password-protected account maintained by the consumer with the business while the consumer is logged into the account as a verifiable consumer request and providing a mechanism for a consumer who does not maintain an account with the business to request information through the business's authentication of the consumer's identity [...][86]

The statute does provide some guidance – for example, if the customer submits both a request and a confirmation through their official account portal while logged in – but there is relatively little guidance for organizations that do not maintain active account profiles for their users, other than putting the onus on the consumer to demonstrate their association with the personal information.[87] Consequently, organizations will need to consider alternative verification mechanisms when handling consumer requests for information, working to complete verification based on the personal data already maintained. The Attorney General's guidance recommends matching either two or three data points provided by the consumer with data points maintained by the business, depending on whether the consumer requests categories of personal information collected or specific pieces of information, along with "a signed declaration under penalty of perjury that the requestor is the

---

[86] Cal. Civ. Code § 1798.185(a)(7).

[87] AG Regulations § 999.325€(2.)

3: The CPRA – key definitions

consumer whose personal information is subject to the request."[88] It may be advisable then for organizations to consider creating dedicated account management portals to help end users effectively manage their own personal information within the organization's systems.

---

[88] AG Regulations § 999.325(b),(c).

CHAPTER 4: ROLES IN THE CPRA: BUSINESSES, BUSINESS PURPOSE, AND SERVICE PROVIDER

Considerable attention has already been given to what constitutes a "business" under the CPRA. As explained, "business" describes covered entities, those organizations primarily responsible for complying, and demonstrating compliance with the CPRA. This responsibility largely hinges on which organization in the data supply chain collects personal information, or directs the means and/or purposes for processing the information. This is similar to the GDPR's understanding of a "data controller."

Under the GDPR, there are both "data controllers" and "data processors." Data processors process personal information on behalf of the data controller, usually based on explicit instruction as outlined in a contract. This situation typically arises in the context of service providers that process data – CRM and enterprise resource planning (ERP) solutions, payroll providers, technology solutions (Cloud offerings, Software as a Service (SaaS), Platform as a Service (PaaS), Logging as a Service (LaaS), etc.). The CPRA sees things similarly, and uses the term "service providers" to describe those organizations "that process information on behalf of a business and which receives from or on behalf of the business a consumer's personal information for a business purpose pursuant to a written contract."[89]

Data processing contracts under the GDPR are governed by Article 28(3), and several things are specifically required.

---

[89] Cal. Civ. Code § 1798.140(ag)(1).

For example, contracts with data processors should include the obligation of confidentiality (i.e. a confidentiality agreement).[90] There must also be relevant security provisions pursuant to Article 32 (technical and organizational measures appropriate to the risk).[91] The CPRA, in contrast, provides relatively little in terms of defined contractual requirements.

The definition of "service provider" in paragraph (ag) explains that the contract with said service provider must prohibit "the person from: (A) selling or sharing the personal information; (B) retaining, using, or disclosing the personal information for any purpose other than for the business purposes specified in the contract for the business." A service provider is also prohibited from "combining the personal information which (it) receives from or on behalf of the business, with personal information which it receives from or on behalf of another person or persons, or collects from its own interaction with the consumer."[92]

Because businesses can disclose a consumer's personal information to a service provider pursuant to a written contract based on a "business purpose," it is critical to understand what "business purpose" is. Disclosing personal information to an organization for something other than a "business purpose" may fall outside the remit of the CPRA's "business" and "service provider" distinction.

---

[90] GDPR Art. 28(3)(b.)

[91] Ibid. at (3)(c).

[92] Cal. Civ. Code § 1798.140(ag)(1)(D).

"Business purpose" generally includes internal, operational uses. Subparagraph (e) outlines what "business purposes" actually are, according to statute.[93]

Business purposes are:

(1) Auditing related to counting ad impressions to unique visitors, verifying positioning and quality of ad impressions, and auditing compliance with this specification and other standards.

(2) Helping to ensure security and integrity to the extent the use of the consumer's personal information is reasonably necessary and proportionate for these purposes.

(3) Debugging to identify and repair errors that impair existing intended functionality.

(4) Short-term, transient use, including but not limited to non-personalized advertising shown as part of a consumer's current interaction with the business, provided that the consumer's personal information is not disclosed to another third party and is not used to build a profile about the consumer or otherwise alter the consumer's experience outside the current interaction with the business.

(5) Performing services on behalf of the business, including maintaining or servicing accounts, providing customer service, processing or fulfilling orders and transactions, verifying customer information,

---

[93] Cal. Civ. Code § 1798.140(e).

processing payments, providing financing, providing analytic services, providing storage, or providing similar services on behalf of the business.

(6) Providing advertising and marketing services, except for cross-context behavioral advertising, to the consumer, provided that for the purpose of advertising and marketing, a service provider or contractor shall not combine the personal information of opted-out consumers which the service provider or contractor receives from or on behalf of the business with personal information with the service provider or contractor receives from or on behalf of another person or persons, or collects from its own interaction with consumers.

(7) Undertaking internal research for technological development and demonstration.

(8) Undertaking activities to verify or maintain the quality or safety of a service or device that is owned, manufactured, manufactured for, or controlled by the business, and to improve, upgrade, or enhance the service or device that is owned, manufactured, manufactured for, or controlled by the business.

Note that this section of statute does not include the phrase "including, but not limited to." It follows then that the list of "business purposes" provided in subparagraph (e) is intended to serve as a complete and final list, as there is no carve-out for possible business purposes currently not under consideration.

In consequence, if any of these activities will be managed by an organization other than the original business, the business will need a contract in place that, at the very least, prohibits the onward organization from processing the personal information for any purpose other than the purpose specifically outlined.

Naturally, both the business and service provider may wish to include other contract terms. For example, the entities could enforce a confidentiality agreement with regard to the personal information, akin to the GDPR. They may also enforce security requirements on each other to help ensure the processing of personal information does not subject any one company to liability based on bad business practices. At the very least, a data processing contract should include an assurance from the service provider that it understands the restrictions as outlined, and will comply with them.

CHAPTER 5: RIGHTS OF CONSUMERS AND OBLIGATIONS OF THE BUSINESS

The CPRA outlines several requirements that apply to a "business." Collectively, this is the operational impact of the CPRA. Although these are often listed as consumer rights, they also impose obligations on a business to allow consumers to exercise those rights.

There are five consumer rights:

1. Right to know and be informed – a right to know what data is being collected, shared, and used, at or before the time of collection.[94]
2. Right of access – a right to have the business disclose various pieces of information related to the data processing.[95]
3. Right to deletion – a right to request that the business delete certain personal information about the consumer.[96]
4. Right to opt-out – a right to request that a business no longer sell or share the consumer's personal information.[97]

---

[94] Cal. Civ. Code § 1798.100, 115.

[95] Cal. Civ. Code § 1798.110.

[96] Cal. Civ. Code § 1798.105.

[97] Cal. Civ. Code § 1798.120.

5. Right to limit use and disclosure of sensitive personal information – consumers have the right to direct a business that collects sensitive personal information to limit its use. Businesses should only be using sensitive personal information when necessary to perform a service or provide goods.[98]

All of these rights take effect in various forms, and the obligations they impose on organizations may seem daunting at first glance. The key here is to understand what each of these rights requires of the organization and how these requirements overlap. With that understanding, the organization can develop reliable, repeatable processes for complying with the CPRA's requirements.

Right of access/right to know and be informed

These similar rights are actually iterated in a few places throughout the CPRA. The first is at the outset – section 100: "A business that controls the collection of consumer's personal information shall, at or before the point of collection, inform consumers as to ..."[99] It is expanded in section 110[100]:

A consumer shall have the right to request that a business that collects personal information disclose the following:

---

[98] Cal. Civ. Code § 1798.121.

[99] Cal. Civ. Code § 1798.100(a).

[100] Cal. Civ. Code § 1798.110(a), (1)–(5).

- The categories of personal information it has collected about that consumer
- The categories of sources from which the personal information is collected
- The business or commercial purpose for collecting or sharing personal information
- The categories of third parties to whom the business discloses personal information
- The specific pieces of personal information it has collected about that consumer

As noted earlier, this same information must be disclosed to a consumer upon receipt of a verifiable consumer request. An easy way to help manage this obligation is simply explaining this information in the organization's privacy notice posted publicly online, and linking or referring to this notice wherever else data is collected.

Other requirements apply relative to the right of access when an organization sells or shares consumers' personal information. These requirements can be found in section 115.

For example, upon receipt of a verifiable consumer request, a business that sells or shares personal information must disclose to the consumer[101]:

- The categories of personal information that the business collected about the consumer

---

[101] Cal. Civ. Code § 1798.115(a), (1)–(3).

- The categories of personal information that the business sold or shared about the consumer
- The categories of third parties to whom the personal information was sold or shared (by category of personal information for each third party)
- The categories of personal information that the business disclosed about the consumer for a business purpose, and the categories of persons to whom it was disclosed

As can be seen, the requirements for organizations that sell personal information are substantially similar to those in sections 100 and 110, which detail the information that must be provided by organizations that simply collect personal information. In either case, organizations processing personal information should be prepared to respond to requests for information relating to the types of information listed above.

Responding to these types of requests will naturally require an innate understanding of an organization's IT infrastructure and business processes. Of course, the front-end parts of the organization that regularly deal with external parties will likely come into play. Marketing, sales, and customer support are usually some of the key business functions that regularly collect, store, share, or sell customers' personal information. These groups also often collect personal information related to sales agents, account managers, and other business contacts as part of their day-to-day work. Although this information is currently exempted from the statute – see Cal. Civil Code § 1798.145(n) – do not neglect this information, especially if those business contacts are California residents (i.e. consumers whose personal information is covered by the CPRA). This may depend on your industry though.

Organizations are often advised to focus on their front-end, external-facing processes and systems first, because these often present a greater risk to the organization than the internal-facing operations. Ideally, internal issues can be handled internally. Any external issues – a concerned customer or media contact – are more likely to be handled externally, by either a regulatory enforcement body (in this case, the California attorney general or the newly created California Privacy Protection Agency) or individual consumers in a civil suit. Internal operations are just as important, however. Administrative functions traditionally managed by human resources or those in a management role typically involve detailed personal information beyond contact identifiers – payroll information, health benefits information, bank accounts, names of spouses and/or children, calendar details, gender, race/ethnicity, criminal backgrounds, etc. This information deserves additional protection based on its sometimes more sensitive nature. That said, a healthy organization should have robust internal reporting mechanisms that handle any complaints efficiently, effectively, respectfully, and internally, before the issue can escalate externally.

Considering the potential operational impact of responding to consumer requests individually, mature organizations should consider a variety of mechanisms to help manage any increased workload related to incoming consumer requests. There are several options available.

Any organization that collects, sells, or shares personal information will have to comply with section 130 of the

CPRA concerning the response to "right of access" requests. This section requires two things:

1. The organization must provide at least two designated methods that allow consumers to submit requests for information, "including, at a minimum, a toll-free telephone number."[102] If the organization maintains a web presence, that website should allow consumers to submit requests for information as well.[103] Organizations that operate directly with consumers and exclusively online are only required to provide an email address.[104]

2. The organization must provide the required information to the consumer free of charge within 45 days of receiving the request.[105] The Attorney General's CCPA Regulations further explain that an organization should confirm receipt within ten days, and "provide information on how the business will process the request," with an expected time frame for response.[106] Although the organization is required to "promptly take steps to determine whether the request is a verifiable

---

[102] Cal. Civ. Code § 1798.130(a)(1)(A).

[103] Cal. Civ. Code § 1798.130(a)(1)(B).

[104] Cal. Civ. Code § 1798.130(a)(1)(A).

[105] Cal. Civ. Code § 1798.130(a)(2)(A).

[106] AG Regulations §999.313(a).

consumer request," requiring reasonable authentication "in light of the nature of the personal information requested," this does not affect the 45-day window.[107] Ultimately, the total time to respond is 45 calendar days after receipt. This period may be extended once, by an additional 45 calendar days, provided the consumer is given notice of the extension within the first 45-day period (90 days maximum total).[108]

For this reason, organizations need to prepare verification mechanisms and corresponding business processes that allow for quick and easy verification of consumer requests. Essentially, organizations need to ensure that the person submitting a request for information is actually the consumer who they claim to be. The importance of this should be obvious – criminal hackers looking to surreptitiously steal personal data should not be able to merely ask for it. A reasonable level of authentication should occur, although the law makes clear that it does not require a business to collect personal information that it would not otherwise collect.[109] Each industry will then have differing requirements for authentication to protect consumers, clients, employees, partners, and business interests. For example, legal services may regularly deal with aggrieved spouses looking for information on recent address changes. Alternatively, investment entities may need to protect geolocation data in case it provides insight into travel related to mergers and

---

[107] AG Regulations §999.313(a).

[108] Ibid.

[109] Cal. Civ. Code § 1798.145(j).

acquisitions. In any case, the organization concerned should consider the context of the industry within which it operates. In addition, the type or sensitivity of the personal information concerned, along with the risk(s) posed to consumers by that information, and the likelihood that malicious actors would seek that information, may impact how stringent the verification process may be.[110] These factors will help provide guidance on the relative level of authentication necessary to process and handle an incoming "right to access" request. Finally, the Attorney General's CCPA guidance advises that a business should never disclose a consumer's Social Security number, driver's license number, financial account number, health/medical identification numbers, or account access information.[111]

Organizations only have to provide information related to the past 12 months (although a consumer may be able to request more than that, in which case a business would need to comply unless it can demonstrate disproportionate effort).[112] The response is to be made in writing, and delivered through either the consumer's account or at the consumer's option (again a compelling reason to consider creating a consumer account portal where requests for information can be collectively tracked and stored, although it should be noted that organizations cannot require a consumer to make an account in order to make a verifiable consumer request).[113]

---

[110] AG Regulations § 999.323(b)(3).

[111] AG Regulations § 999.313(c)(4).

[112] Cal. Civ. Code § 1798.130(a)(2)(B).

[113] Cal. Civ. Code § 1798.130(a)(2)(A).

Organizations are also not obligated to reply to the same consumer request more than twice in a 12-month period.[114]

Curiously, there is wording buried in subparagraph (a)(2) of section 130 that contains language similar to the GDPR's "right to data portability." Article 20 of the GDPR states:

> The data subject shall have the right to receive the personal data concerning him or her [...] in a structured, commonly used and machine-readable format and have the right to transmit those data to another controller without hindrance [...][115]

The CPRA, meanwhile, requires responses to verifiable consumer requests to be provided "in a readily useable format that allows the consumer to transmit this information from one entity to another entity without hindrance."[116] Considering this requirement applies to both categories and specific pieces of information, organizations must be able to respond completely to consumer requests, which means that they must be able to identify and gather the necessary information, and provide it to the consumer in the appropriate format.

This will likely require data mapping or data flow audits that help track what data is collected from consumers, how that data is used, and where it is stored. In turn, this will help personnel reply to verifiable consumer requests, because

---

[114] Cal. Civ. Code § 1798.130(b).

[115] GDPR, Article 20(1).

[116] Cal. Civ. Code § 1798.130(a)(2)(A).

they will ideally have access to a controlled repository where they can quickly filter and search for key data elements related to a consumer, along with additional information related to the organization's use or intended business purpose for the data.

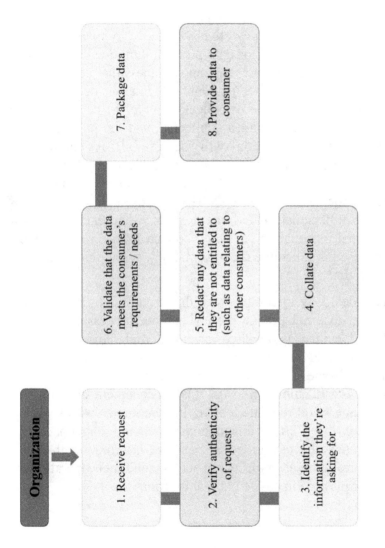

Figure 1: An example of an organization's data subject access request process

Privacy notices

Section 130 of the CPRA outlines some other obligations. As is likely imaginable, many of the aforementioned requirements can be proactively managed by maintaining a public privacy policy or data processing notice. Remember that section 100 requires that any business that controls the collection of consumer personal information must inform consumers at the time of collection as to the categories of personal information to be collected, and the purposes for which the information will be used.[117] As a result, organizations will already need to prepare some kind of public privacy policy or data processing notice based on the requirements in section 100. That is, any organization that collects personal data must explain what categories of personal information are being collected, and why (i.e. the purpose for collecting the information), at the time of actual collection.

The ideal way to comply with this section is to maintain a single, external privacy policy or data processing notice. This document is prepared for an external audience, and is whitewashed of any company proprietary information or internal trade secrets. This is the document that gets posted to the organization's website; it is the document shared with consumers and regulators alike. In compliance with section 100 of the CPRA, this document should explain, at a minimum, the categories of personal information that an organization collects from consumers, and their operational use or purpose in collecting that information.

---

[117] Cal. Civ. Code § 1798.100(a)(1).

Section 100 makes clear that this document, or more generally, this notice of information to be collected, should be provided at or before the "point of collection" – that is, before the information is collected, or at the actual time of collection.[118] For example, some organizations may maintain a process whereby data is collected – an online form with static or dynamic data collection fields – which is when this privacy policy or data processing notice should be provided to the user.

Data can, of course, be collected by other methods as well: paper forms, telephone calls, email outreach, etc. An organization may wish to prepare its data privacy notice in respect to specific data collection processes if each of those processes is sufficiently distinct enough to warrant a separate notice. However, the actual management of those notices may become a burden unto itself. Collaborative authoring, version control, publishing authority, and other aspects of corporate communications will need to be managed for each individual policy document that describes the data processing activities concerned. For large organizations, this can easily create a cumbersome and unrealistic approach to managing notices and access.

Organizations have a variety of disclosure obligations as well, set out in sections 100, 110, and 115 of the CPRA. These disclosures are usually in response to a consumer request, but sometimes exist as general requirements. Ideally then, rather than maintaining separate processes focused on each individual aspect of compliance, organizations will consider a holistic approach to compliance – a programmatic

---

[118] Cal. Civ. Code § 1798.100(a).

model, as opposed to a "check-the-box" initiative. Again, it is important to understand each individual part of the CPRA to help fully grasp it as a whole.

A holistic approach to CPRA compliance will weave together various interrelated parts of the statute. In this case, these will be the requirements related to notice, disclosure, and access. Mature organizations will start to comply by first engaging in data mapping or data flow activities to find out exactly what information they collect, for what purpose, and with whom that information may also be shared.

Once the full data lifecycle is understood internally, only then can it be explained externally. Ideally, this should be done in a single data privacy policy or processing notice. Rather than maintaining separate documents to describe separate data processing activities, organizations should aim to outline and explain their entire data processing model in a single document or small series of documents (or at least as much as is appropriate for public consumption). This will help centralize coordination and control over this single "master document" that outlines all practices relevant to personal data and privacy. The master document can then be shared as necessary, ideally via a link, so that all personnel access and refer to the same source of truth as a matter of practice. This helps eliminate the confusion sometimes associated with document management in a corporate context – who made which revisions, whether a document is suitable for external release, what version is the correct version, etc. Where data is actually collected by the organization, subsequent web pages or forms can link to the original policy document, which should also live as a standalone page on the organization's web platform – usually under a commonly used title, such as "Privacy" or "Privacy Policy," or "Your Privacy Rights."

From there, organizations will need to consider the format and structure of this policy document. The policy should be structured in a way that is not overly confusing to average consumers. That is, the document should be written clearly, with commonly used terms that minimize the use of industry slang or legal jargon. Statements that outline data processing practices should aim to provide clarity, with direct sentences that avoid unclear, qualifying language (e.g. "sometimes," "we may," "in certain circumstances"). Paragraphs and sentences should be appropriately grouped so that it is clear which products, services, or activities collect and process which personal information for which purposes. The average person should be able to readily navigate to the organization's privacy policy, read the policy with minimal issue or confusion, and walk away with a relatively clear understanding of what personal data processing looks like at the organization. It is also important to note that the Attorney General's CCPA Regulations require that the privacy notice be reasonably accessible to consumers with disabilities (see Web Content Accessibility Guidelines, version 2.1 of June 5, 2018, from the World Wide Web Consortium). Clearly, some time should be spent determining what exactly is included in this policy document. Some organizations may find it useful to look at publicly available privacy policies to get a sense of how others in their industry have approached the structure and format of the policy or notice.

The data privacy policy or data processing notice must include the following:

YOUR RIGHTS - A description of consumer rights, pursuant to Sections 1798.100 (access/notice), 1798.105 (deletion), 1798.106 (correcting inaccurate information), 1798.110 (access/request for data), 1798.115 (access/request for shared or sold data), and 1798.125 (non-discrimination).[119]

Often, organizations will list those rights in their policy documents, along with instructions for how to submit a verifiable consumer request (e.g. links to a form, or contact information for the company's privacy officer). Further explanation of which consumer's rights apply in an individual scenario can be managed via the "verifiable consumer request" (i.e. outreach) mechanism.

One important note: A business that sells or shares personal information will also be required to notify consumers that they have a right to "opt-out" of the selling or sharing of their personal information (along with a "Do Not Sell or Share My Personal Information" button).[120] If the business discloses sensitive personal information for any purposes other than that which is strictly necessary, the business will be required to post a link titled "Limit the Use of My Sensitive Personal Information."[121] If the business does not sell or share consumer information, it should state that it does not and will

---

[119] Cal. Civ. Code § 1798.130(a)(5)(A).

[120] Cal. Civ. Code § 1798.135(a)(1).

[121] Cal. Civ. Code § 1798.135(a)(1).

not sell or share personal information in the privacy policy.[122]

HOW TO ENFORCE THEM - A description of the method for submitting verifiable consumer requests.[123]

Typically, organizations will maintain a point-of-contact email address for handling issues related to data privacy, cybersecurity, and data governance. This email inbox may be managed by a single person, such as a data privacy officer or chief compliance officer. Alternatively, it may be handled by a team or department. The person or persons may just be responsible for responding to consumers, or they may also manage the entire privacy compliance program. The internal structure and associated processes are of less relevance at this stage; what is important is that the organization's privacy policy does maintain a point of communication, generally via email, whereby privacy issues and consumer privacy rights are managed. It should be enough that organizations outline the rights enumerated by the CPRA, and simply point consumers to the correct contact for more information or explanation of those rights. Organizations must also generally describe the process they will use to verify the consumer's identity in order to proceed with the request. Do not forget though – the organization must make a toll-free telephone number available for the exercising of some rights (or an email address) – see section 130(a)(1)(A) – so in reality, a CPRA privacy policy will likely include contact information for an organization's privacy manager in both

---

[122] Cal. Civ. Code § 1798.115(c)(1), (2).

[123] Cal. Civ. Code § 1798.130(a)(5)(A).

email and telephone format, unless the organization works directly with consumers exclusively online.

DATA WE COLLECT - A list of categories of personal information collected about consumers in the preceding 12 months.[124]

For guidance on listing categories of information, consider the categorical groupings listed in section 140(v)(1): identifiers, protected classes, commercial information, biometric information, education information, employment information, location data, etc.

WHERE THE DATA COMES FROM - The categories of sources from which personal information is collected.[125]

This is an explanation of how the organization got hold of the consumer's personal information. For example, some organizations may only act as service providers, in which case it would be beneficial to explain which organization in the data supply chain acted as the "business" that originally collected the data (and thus, the organization that is often ultimately responsible for responding to consumers). In some industries, it is also common for organizations to share or purchase information, such as mailing lists or other contact details.

---

[124] Cal. Civ. Code § 1798.100(a)(1); *see also* § 1798.130(a)(5)(B), referencing § 1798.110(c). referencing § 1798.130(a)(5)(B).

[125] Cal. Civ. Code § 1798.130(a)(5)(B).

WHAT WE DO WITH IT - The business or commercial purpose for collecting, using, selling or sharing the personal information.[126]

Organizations often indicate the nature of the function using the information concerned. For example, contact details may be used for outreach and engagement, commercial information may be used for sales and marketing, network activity information may be used as a part of service provision or for license compliance, additional identifiers may be used for verification, etc.

As may become clear, there are similar but separate requirements that apply to organizations that sell personal information, as opposed to those that merely collect information. Section 135 deals with the notice and disclosure requirements that apply to these types of organizations. In addition, organizations that sell consumer personal information to third parties will need to concern themselves with the "right to opt-out."

HOW LONG WE STORE IT - The length of time the business intends to retain each category of personal information.[127]

If it is not possible to outline the retention periods that apply to the personal information, the business can instead list the criteria that would be used to determine such periods.

---

[126] Cal. Civ. Code § 1798.100(a)(1); *see also* § 1798.130(a)(5)(B).

[127] Cal. Civil Code § 1798,100(a)(3).

WHO ELSE WE GIVE IT TO - The categories of third parties to whom the business discloses personal information.[128]

Along with an understanding of what the organization concerned does with personal information, consumers should also be able to easily understand where the data came from, and where else it might go. Transparency is a key theme underlying many international data protection and privacy regimes, so it is only natural to see that same element enshrined in the CPRA. Rather than responding to individual customer requests on this topic, it is likely easier for an organization to explain the nature of its third-party data processors (service providers and/or contractors) at the outset of data collection. This can help minimize the burden associated with verifiable consumer requests.

The Attorney General's CCPA Regulations include the following list of "categories of third parties": advertising networks, Internet service providers, data analytics providers, government entities, operating systems and platforms, social networks, and data brokers.[129]

If the organization does not sell, share, or disclose consumer personal information, it should say so in its privacy policy.[130]

---

[128] Cal. Civil Code § 1798,130(a)(5)(B), referencing § 1798.110(c).

[129] AG Regulations – Section 999.301(E).

[130] Cal. Civ. Code § 1798.115(c)(1), (2).

WHAT WE GIVE THEM - A list of categories of personal information that are sold or shared, and/or a list of categories of information that are disclosed for a business purpose.[131]

Organizations may wish to consider how this will be presented and explained in the privacy policy. Does it make sense to group data collection activities by product or service? What about activities involving the onward transfer of data? There is no correct approach here, and the final style used will depend largely on the organization and the complexity of its data processing activities. Ultimately, though, the reader should not find it difficult to understand what data is being collected, for what purpose, and who else may receive that data, whenever the customer uses the product or service at issue.

Note that as it applies to the policy document, the list of categories of personal information collected or sold, or shared or disclosed applies only to the preceding 12 months.[132] Consequently, the organization is responsible for updating information contained in the policy at least once every 12 months.[133]

To manage this, organizations will need to consider review and revision processes for the policy. Senior management should be involved in an annual process to review the policy document itself, while stakeholders from various business functions should be allowed to inject input in real time. This

---

[131] Cal. Civ. Code§ 1798.130(a)(5)(C), referencing § 1798.115(c).

[132] Cal. Civ. Code § 1798.130(a)(5)(B) and (C).

[133] Cal. Civ. Code § 1798.130(a)(5).

allows any day-to-day changes to be captured immediately if they have a privacy impact, whereas other process changes that do not heavily impact privacy can be reviewed on a periodic basis. The review process should include change management methodologies to help ensure all relevant parties are aware of what has changed versus what has stayed the same. Invariably, the policy's publication date should be updated annually as well.

Considering the amount of information that must be included in an organization's privacy policy, and given the considerable back-end processes required to update and disseminate the policy, mature organizations should consider adding some extra information to their public-facing policies. This additional information does not necessarily need to be published in the policy itself, but organizations are variously required to disclose this information as part of other statutory provisions. As a result, organizations may prefer to pre-emptively disclose some additional pieces of information within their privacy policy or processing notice, rather than having to give this information out in response to each individual consumer request.

Data privacy policies or data processing notices should explain the following:

Specific pieces of personal information that are collected, sold, and/or disclosed.

The requirement to list categories of information collected comes from section 130, and relates to compliance with section 110, which also discusses the disclosure of specific pieces of personal information collected (*see* § 1798.110(c)(5), which gives consumers the right to request what specific pieces of personal information have been collected). As a result, in addition to listing the categories of information collected, organizations may wish to explain what specific pieces of information constitute those categories, likely in an effort to help consumers understand more clearly what data is involved. By outlining this information in the privacy notice, ideally organizations can reduce the volume of consumer requests for information, as it is already publicly posted.

Right to opt-out

This is the right to request that a business that sells or shares personal information to third parties no longer sell or share the consumer's personal information.[134]

Organizations engaged in selling or sharing consumer personal information will face compliance challenges slightly different from those organizations that merely collect and process personal information for their own use. Disclosure requirements for these organizations can be found in section 115 of the CPRA, although they substantially mirror the disclosure requirements outlined previously (i.e. full transparency around the data lifecycle). In addition, these organizations will need to comply with the "right to opt-out" found in section 120, which in turn dictates what must be included in the public privacy policy per section 135.

To start, consumers have the right to direct a business that sells or shares their personal information to stop selling or sharing this information at any time.[135] This is the "right to

---

[134] Cal. Civ. Code § 1798.120.

[135] Cal. Civ. Code § 1798.120(a).

opt-out." Businesses that sell personal information to third parties are required to notify consumers that their information may be sold or shared, and that they have a right to opt-out of this activity.[136] Businesses that sell the information of minors face an additional hurdle, because consumers who are between ages 13–16 must give affirmative authorization to sell their personal information.[137] According to the Attorney General's CCPA Regulations, "affirmative authorization" is defined as "an action that demonstrates the intentional decision by the consumer to opt-in," and can involve a two-step process for minors between 13 and 16 years of age, or some level of parental/guardian consent.[138]

Before moving forward, organizations need to pause to consider what happens if a consumer does opt-out (or, for minors, if the consumer does not opt-in):

1. Can the technology concerned actually be manipulated to pause or stop the onward transfer of the information?
2. Are there any primary or secondary business processes that would be impacted by this interruption?

Organizations are often structured around efficient hand-offs between one group and the next. Are these groups so tightly controlled that a consumer request can be effectively handled

---

[136] Cal. Civ. Code § 1798.120(b).

[137] This right may be referred to as the "right to opt-in"; *see* Cal. Civ. Code § 1798.120(c).

[138] AG Regulations § 999.301(a).

by one unit? Or does responsibility need to be allocated among the different groups involved:

- Those who are accountable for responding to opt-out requests;
- Those who need to be consulted or contacted; and
- Third parties that may also rely on this data?

How will that sale be affected? It is often useful to consider the full lifecycle of the personal information involved, from data collection to storage to disposal, in order to understand all the touchpoints inside and outside the organization.

Once this is complete, attention and energy can be turned to developing supplemental processes that do not rely on the data transfer. Remember that an organization that sells or shares personal information not only needs to manage consumer requests to opt-out as a process itself (i.e. outreach mechanism, responding within the proper time frame, documenting responses for compliance audit, passing on those requests internally to other functions, etc.) but also the effects of the process. How will the organization respond when consumers stop granting permission for the onward transfer of data? Can permission be granted based on a smaller scope of data? Are alternative arrangements in place should a consumer completely remove their permissions? In short, organizations that rely on the sale or sharing of consumer personal information may face an existential crisis if consumers stop supporting their data processing activities.

Unlike the GDPR, consumers do not need to actively opt-in to data-selling arrangements under the CPRA, and organizations may be able to continue dealing in personal data without the consent of the consumer. However, smart organizations will prepare for eventualities that do not involve data sale, assuming that at least some consumers will permanently exercise their right to opt-out when the statute takes effect. This may present daunting, long-term structural challenges for organizations that rely heavily on revenue from selling data. Procedurally, though, the remainder of the CPRA is relatively straightforward on what is required in terms of notice and disclosure.

Of course, any organization that sells or shares personal information to third parties must disclose to consumers that the information may be sold or shared, and that they have a right to opt-out of this activity. Section 135 goes on to require that this disclosure be provided via "a clear and conspicuous link on the business's Internet homepage, titled 'Do Not Sell or Share My Personal Information.'"[139] Consumers should be able to use this page to directly opt-out of the selling or sharing of their personal information via an interactive web page, on top of the email or telephone mechanism available. Organizations must also include a description of the right to opt-out along with a separate link to this page in its online privacy policies.[140] So, what does this look like in practice?

Much like the disclosure requirements explained above, organizations that sell or share personal information should consider a holistic approach to compliance. Rather than maintaining several different links on a web page (each possibly with its own process), a single privacy policy that outlines the right to opt-out in detail may be preferable. That master policy can pay a great deal of attention to the mechanisms that enable customers to exercise this right. For

---

[139] Cal. Civ. Code § 1798.135(a)(1).

[140] Cal. Civ. Code § 1798.135(a)(1)–(3).

example, some organizations may be able to offer self-service tools that allow consumers to opt-out at their leisure – although note that organizations cannot compel consumers to create an account purely for the purposes of exercising this right (the issue then being whether the organization can actually function based on the unpredictable whims of consumers opting into and out of the sale of their information). Other organizations may maintain a separate opt-out process, or treat this request no different from any other verifiable consumer request that comes in via email or telephone.

Regardless of the actual way consumers can opt-out, the idea is that all detail relevant to this right lives in the same master policy document, thereby streamlining the management and review of the policy and its related sub-processes. Organizations could put clear and conspicuous links across their web presence that read "Do Not Sell or Share My Personal Information," and use this link to direct the consumer to the privacy policy (perhaps linking directly to the applicable section of the policy), rather than creating a separate web page. The goal is to minimize the amount of tangential processes that need ongoing maintenance and review. Ideally, everything related to privacy should be linked together.

Once a consumer opt-outs of the onward sale or sharing of their information, the organization must refrain from selling the information within 15 days[141], and for at least 12 months.[142] After 12 months, the organization can reach out

---

[141] AG Regulations § 999.313(e).

[142] Cal. Civ. Code § 1798.135(a)(4).

to the consumer to request permission to sell or share the personal information again.[143]

Right to deletion

This is the right to request that a business delete any personal information about the consumer that the business collected.[144]

Nowhere does the issue of inner workings become clearer than with regard to the right to deletion. Section 105 of the CPRA broadly states: "A consumer shall have the right to request that a business delete any personal information about the consumer which the business has collected from the consumer."[145] Regulatory guidance from the Attorney General indicates that a two-step process is required, whereby a consumer must submit a request for deletion, and then separately confirm deletion.[146] The business should also explain that it will retain a record of the request.[147]

Businesses collecting personal information must, of course, disclose this right to deletion, and thus the privacy policy may be an ideal place to disclose all consumer privacy rights generally. This way, all privacy rights are consistently explained to all consumers, regardless of whether the right

---

[143] Cal. Civ. Code § 1798.135(a)(4).

[144] Cal. Civ. Code § 1798.105.

[145] Cal. Civ. Code § 1798.105(a).

[146] AG Regulations §999.312(d).

[147] AG Regulations §999.313(d)(5).

actually applies to the data concerned – something that can be analyzed, and explained, via the consumer response process.

The right to deletion is not absolute – the organization can continue to hold a consumer's personal information if it is necessary for a number of purposes. The CPRA recognizes there may be situations where organizations cannot realistically delete data.

Neither a business nor a service provider needs to comply with a request for deletion if the information is needed to [148]:

"Complete the transaction for which the personal information was collected, fulfill the terms of a written warranty or product recall conducted in accordance with federal law, provide a good or service requested by the consumer, or reasonably anticipated by the consumer within the context of a business' ongoing business relationship with the consumer, or otherwise perform a contract between the business and the consumer."[149]

This applies where the information to be deleted is necessary to complete the original transaction. For example, a customer's contact details are likely needed to provide a product or service, and cannot be realistically deleted mid-transaction. How would the customer actually receive what they paid for? In contrast, many organizations use their existing sales funnels as a marketing or reselling channel. If

---

[148] Cal. Civ. Code § 1798.105(d)(1)–(8).

[149] Cal. Civ. Code § 1798.105(d)(1).

an organization is currently using information in furtherance of product or process *A*, and the customer has requested deletion with regard to product or process *B*, the organization needs to be able to segregate the information to comply with the consumer's request. This will help ensure that a single request for deletion does not inadvertently cause the deletion of all personal information related to that consumer. If the consumer still requests the information be deleted at the end of the transaction, that request should be honored (as there is no articulated business purpose for keeping or using the data anymore).

"Help to ensure security and integrity to the extent the use of the consumer's personal information is reasonably necessary and proportionate for those purposes."[150]

This is especially relevant in the context of electronic information and logs. Good cybersecurity inherently requires accurate system logs to determine who accessed what system, when. Often this information cannot or should not be deleted. Some organizations may also track IP addresses or device IDs to help manage licenses for software and SaaS offerings. This information does not need to be deleted simply because a consumer requests deletion. However, the organization will need to understand precisely which data elements are used for which business purpose (e.g. completing a transaction versus security management). This will make it clearer to personnel why certain information is needed (and, consequently, how it is intended to be used at the organization). By making this information clear, those responsible for responding to consumer requests for deletion

---

[150] Cal. Civ. Code § 1798.105(d)(2).

can more quickly and easily identify which information is suitable for deletion, and which cannot (or should not) be deleted.

"Debug to identify and repair errors that impair existing intended functionality."[151]

This exception only applies to debugging efforts used in the identification and repair of existing functionality. This does not carve out a broad exception for organizations to hold personal information for future research and development projects; it only applies to active issues.

"Exercise free speech."[152]

This exception allows an organization to hold consumer personal information for the purposes of exercising free speech, or another right provided by law. Presumably this is focused on the rights of the organization, as it may be hard to imagine a scenario where a consumer requests the deletion of their information, and in turn the organization replies that the information cannot be deleted because the information helps the consumer exercise their own rights (presumably, if a consumer was using personal information to exercise their free speech, they would not request that the information be deleted, as they would no longer be exercising their right). It also specifies ensuring the right of another consumer to exercise their right of free speech.

This may be particularly relevant for news organizations, media outlets, and social media companies. Keep in mind

---

[151] Cal. Civ. Code § 1798.105(d)(3).

[152] Cal. Civ. Code § 1798.105(d)(4).

that the definition of personal information under the CPRA includes broad language: "information that identifies, relates to, describes, is reasonably capable of being associated with, or could reasonably be linked, directly or indirectly, with a particular consumer or household." As a result, comments posted on a news board or web forum could be considered personal information (personal information includes information regarding a consumer's interaction with an Internet website – see § 1798.140(v)(1)(F)). For example, if someone posts a comment about the Governor of California on the web page of a news article, that comment would theoretically contain the Governor's personal information (i.e. name). If the Governor attempted to exercise a right to delete that information, the news outlet could perhaps claim a free speech exemption. However, organizations engaged in those industries should review relevant bodies of law related to constitutional guarantees of free speech in order to more clearly define what constitutes "exercising" this right.

"Engage in public or peer-reviewed scientific, historical, or statistical research that conforms or adheres to all other applicable ethics and privacy laws".[153]

This exception comes with a few caveats. First, the research must adhere to all other applicable ethics and privacy laws (e.g. HIPAA for research involving personal health information).

Second, the research exception only applies if deleting the information concerned would seriously impair the research. That is, if the scientific, historical, or statistical research can continue unimpacted by the loss of consumer personal

---

[153] Cal. Civ. Code § 1798.105(d)(6).

information, it can (and should) be deleted upon request. Personal information could also be deidentified, so that the raw research data is still useful while preserving consumers' privacy. As a result, organizations looking to avail themselves of this exception will need to prepare for rebuttals to possible claims that the information can be deleted with minimal impact. Should an organization argue that it must retain consumer personal information for research purposes, it should be prepared to show how that personal information is vital to the research.

Finally, this exception only applies if the consumer has provided consent.[154] Therefore, in order to reject a request for deletion because the organization needs the information for research, the organization will likely need to demonstrate that the information is vital for research to continue, and that the consumer understands and consents. In effect, the consumer is basically consenting for their personal information to continue to be used – otherwise, without consent, it is unlikely the organization can continue using the information.

"Comply with a legal obligation."[155]

This relates to a true legal obligation, not some policy, code of conduct, or industry standard. Should an organization wish to avail itself of this exception, it should be able to point to a specific statute, law, or official document (e.g. warrant, subpoena, etc.) that outlines the requirements relating to personal information.

---

[154] Cal. Civ. Code § 1798.105(d)(6).

[155] Cal. Civ. Code § 1798.105(d)(8).

That said, there are many scenarios in which data must be retained for legal reasons. Tax laws often require certain information to be saved for a period of time; contracts may also contain specific stipulations regarding data retention. Ideally, organizations should maintain a list or register of all their legal obligations, as it can be useful to understand and analyze their evolving impact on the organization as a whole.

"To enable solely internal uses that are reasonably aligned with the expectations of the consumer based on the consumer's relationship with the business."[156]

This is an exception that allows for internal operations. Under the exception outlined here, it should not be an issue to share consumer information within the same silo, product, or business area, as long as those internal uses are "reasonably aligned with the expectations of the consumer."

For example, many organizations rely on existing customers for potential upsell or resell revenue. Most customers will likely expect a bit of material to be sent their way with regard to existing products or services (e.g. software updates, hardware upgrades). It should also be reasonable for them to expect their personal information to be used in furtherance of the overall business relationship – account management, invoicing, technical support, etc.

It may be unreasonable to reach across silos or areas and share information. Consumers who purchase laptops expect to hear more about laptops – they likely do not expect or want to hear more about other devices (if they did, they would have indicated this). Again, it is crucial to understand what

---

[156] Cal. Civ. Code § 1798.105(d)(7).

data is being used for exactly what purpose. Data processing activities need to be kept separate – ideally, each data element or information identifier is being used for one business purpose at a time. That way, functions across the organization can be clear about why the information is in use for each individual process, which in turn helps provide clarity on what data can be deleted (and who is responsible for that).

Any organization that receives a valid request for deletion must actually delete the consumer's personal information.[157] This may seem obvious, but the key is in demonstrating compliance. How can an organization prove it has deleted personal information if the personal information no longer exists? Organizations need to therefore consider the various documentation requirements associated with verifiable consumer requests, to help demonstrate that the actions taken by the organization actually did occur, and they did so in accordance with the law and within the right time frame. In this case, records of deletion could be maintained. Not an actual record of the information concerned, but rather, a record of what was deleted (e.g. "[Consumer name]'s contact details were deleted on XXX date in response to consumer request received on YYY date."). Ideally, this is all tied to the consumer response process, as it is likely that many different types of consumer requests will come through that channel. Track them all and document them appropriately. However, each issue will need to be dealt with individually based on the consumer and the information involved.

---

[157] Cal. Civ. Code § 1798.105(c).

Another procedural hurdle for organizations to consider comes with the onward notice of a deletion request. Organizations will need to notify any associated service providers to also delete the requested information from their records.[158] Consequently, organizations need to prepare notification mechanisms along the data supply chain as it relates to consumer information, along with associated contractual requirements that will flow out to service providers. Once a request is received and verified by the business, internal mechanisms should kick-off a notification process that advises associated service providers of the verified request (for their own compliance documentation) and the information requested to be deleted.

In turn, the service provider should notify the business that the request has been filled, either in writing or through some other certification process that indicates the deletion request was honored. Organizations may wish to impose time limits on when a service provider must respond to and/or honor a deletion request, so that the service provider's actions do not pose a liability to the business (for example, what if a business honors a consumer's request for deletion but the service provider does not? Who is at fault for the continued use of the information? Can the original organization prove it provided instructions for deletion to the service provider? Can the service provider prove the request was honored?). Much of compliance comes down to following documented processes and keeping records that demonstrate this – it is not just about following the law, but following the law in

---

[158] Cal. Civ. Code § 1798.105(c).

such a way that proves the organization continually manages its operations according to compliant practices.

There are, of course, technical considerations. First, can this actually be done? Can consumer information actually be deleted? Discussions with IT, systems engineers, database managers, and software developers will likely be key at this stage. Some tools and systems either cannot, or may not have been configured to, cleanly delete data on a point-by-point basis.

If deletion is not technically possible, are other deidentification methods available? Remember that the CPRA does not restrict the collection, use, retention, storage, or disclosure of consumer information that is either deidentified or in the aggregate,[159] so there may be workarounds if the information cannot be deleted but can otherwise be completely stripped of its identifying characteristics. This might include, for instance, certain types of encryption, especially if it can be made irreversible (such as by deleting or destroying the encryption key).

Right to no retaliation

Organizations cannot discriminate against a consumer simply because the consumer exercised their rights under the CPRA.[160] For example, an organization cannot deny goods or services, or provide a different quality of goods or services in an attempt to discourage consumers from exercising their

---

[159] Cal. Civ. Code § 1798.145(a)(6).

[160] Cal. Civ. Code § 1798.125(a).

rights.[161] However, an organization can charge different prices or provide different levels of services to a consumer who has exercised their rights, as long as that difference is "reasonably related to the value provided to the business by the consumer's data."[162] In addition, organizations may offer financial incentives as compensation "for the collection of personal information, the sale or sharing of personal information, or the retention of personal information" (although the consumer must give opt-in consent, which must be revocable at any time).[163]

Summary

Organizations must prepare a variety of internal and external-facing processes to ensure they comply with their new obligations. Covered entities need to consider a method that allows consumers to submit requests for information or deletion (including, at a minimum, a toll-free phone number, and if the business maintains a website, a web address).[164] Responses to such requests (called "data subject access requests," or "DSARs" in the EU) must be delivered free of charge within 45 calendar days (confirming receipt within 10 days).[165] Much like the GDPR, that time period can be extended under certain circumstances, provided the

---

[161] Cal. Civ. Code § 1798.125(a)(1).

[162] Cal. Civ. Code § 1798.125(a)(2).

[163] Cal. Civ. Code § 1798.125(b).

[164] Cal. Civ. Code § 1798.130(a)(1).

[165] Cal. Civ. Code § 1798.130(a)(2)(A).

organization gives notice to the consumer.[166] Additionally, disclosures must be made "in a readily useable format that allows the consumer to transmit this information from one entity to another entity without hindrance."[167] All of these things will require an innate understanding of the organization and its data processing activities in order to provide transparency into those activities (i.e. notice and disclosure). Furthermore, organizations must simultaneously prepare for the procedural impact of these new consumer rights, not only in terms of actually managing and replying to consumer requests but also in the related internal inner workings.

As an organization tackles the procedural hurdles associated with consumer notice, disclosure, opt-out, and deletion requests, it will need to consider the substantive hurdles as well. As discussed earlier, what happens if a consumer requests that their information is no longer sold or shared? How does that actually impact a business that relies on data sales for revenue? Similarly, what happens if a consumer requests that their information be deleted?

The clearest solution is to establish clear, public-facing information about processing and consumers' rights, and to link this to simple methods for exercising those rights. The organization can then digest requests so that they can be directed to the correct parts of the business, each of which should have clear processes for complying with requests,

---

[166] Cal. Civ. Code § 1798.130(a)(2)(A).

[167] Ibid.

which can then be compiled centrally and any necessary responses can be directed to the consumer.

CHAPTER 6: SECURITY REQUIREMENTS

"Data security" is mentioned as a topic in the CPRA first in section 100(E):

> A business that collects a consumer's personal information shall implement reasonably security procedures and practices appropriate to the nature of the personal information to protect (it) from unauthorized or illegal access, destruction, use, modification, or disclosure.

Note that this references another section of the California Civil Code, which will be discussed later: Section 1798.81.5.

Security is also found in section 150. That section actually contains what is left of the original ballot proposal's private right of action, and it details how consumers can make a claim under the CPRA. In turn, some insight can be gained into the obligations of organizations, and how they can rebut consumer claims.

At the time of writing, consumers will only be able to institute a civil action against an organization for failure to secure data. Such a claim actually has several requirements under section 150. First, the personal information must be "nonencrypted and nonredacted."[168] So, an easy way for organizations to avoid liability under this section – and thus, perhaps a security suggestion, if not an outright requirement – is to simply encrypt all consumer personal information.

---

[168] Cal. Civ. Code § 1798.150(a)(1).

Note, however, that "nonencrypted and nonredacted personal information" are defined in this section by virtue of reference to subparagraph (A) of paragraph (1) of subdivision (d) of section 1798.81.5 of the California Civil Code, which technically does not live in the CPRA itself. Somewhat curiously then, the legislative drafters of the CPRA have chosen to redefine "personal information" for this purpose. Again it can be seen that great care must be taken when reading parts of a statute in order to understand how all the parts fit together.

"Personal information," for purposes of a consumer civil suit under section 150, must then meet the definition outlined in section 81.5. There, "personal information" means either of the following[169]:

(1)

    (A) An individual's first name or first initial and his or her last name in combination with any one or more of the following data elements, when either the name or the data elements are not encrypted or redacted:

        (i)   Social Security number.

        (ii) Driver's license number or California identification card number.

        (iii) Account number, credit or debit card number, in combination with any required security code, access code, or password that would permit access to an individual's financial account.

---

[169] Cal. Civ. Code § 1798.81.5(d)(1)–(3).

(iv) Medical information.

(v) Health insurance information.

(B) A username or email address in combination with a password or security question and answer that would permit access to an online account.

(2) "Medical information" means any individually identifiable information, in electronic or physical form, regarding the individual's medical history or medical treatment or diagnosis by a health care professional.

(3) "Health insurance information" means an individual's insurance policy number or subscriber identification number, any unique identifier used by a health insurer to identify the individual, or any information in an individual's application and claims history, including any appeals records.

As can be seen, this definition of "personal information" is slightly narrower than the definition provided in section 140 (almost anything that can directly or indirectly link, relate to, or be associated with a consumer). As a result, organizations should take special care to safeguard this information – in particular, Social Security numbers, identification card numbers, account numbers and payment information, medical information, and health insurance information – likely by means of encryption, or redaction where possible.

So, as it relates to security requirements under the CPRA – organizations have a "duty to implement and maintain reasonable security procedures and practices appropriate to the nature of the information."[170] Generally speaking, the

---

[170] Cal. Civ. Code § 1798.150(a)(1).

security obligations imposed on organizations by the CPRA are really about maintaining "reasonable security." The idea is that applied security controls may differ depending on the organization and the data concerned. It is unlikely that all data will be treated the same for security purposes, so the law is specifically written to provide only a duty of maintaining "reasonable security." What is considered "reasonable" is then left to the organization.

Any organization in the middle of a data governance project should truly consider a risk-based approach to project initiation, program development, and ongoing maintenance. This approach balances the risks to the information, the organization, and the consumer against the practicalities of securing the information. This allows the organization to define what it considers "reasonable security," which it can amend in later reviews if it finds that security measures are ineffective or impractical, or that security is excessively strict. Through an ongoing process of review and correction, the organization can develop a streamlined, effective, and "reasonable" set of security measures.

Different security controls are applied to different systems and databases – there likely is not a one-size-fits-all approach. Unfortunately, tailor-made systems are difficult to assess for liability purposes. If an issue were to arise, litigation may inevitably devolve into a battle of the experts, whereby one IT guru argues that the security is reasonable, while another IT guru argues that the security was not reasonable at all. Essentially, it becomes difficult to pin down what was reasonable in the circumstances unless there is a systematic model for compliance based on objective risk analysis. Otherwise, the organization will be left arguing (at considerable cost) why its approach was reasonable in that particular instance.

A risk-based approach to IT security management allows the organization to rely on its compliance program – a combination of people, process, and technology-driven solutions – to provide a model for consistent approaches to risk analysis and remediation. The organization ideally will not have to argue why its approach was reasonable in any given instance. Rather, it can argue that its program delivers a model for compliance based on risk. The idea is no different from grade school math – there is value in showing how one arrived at the answer, in addition to the answer itself.

Processes are often easier to analyze for compliance purposes than ad hoc activities because they exist as semi-stable templates. This is the benefit of risk management or risk control frameworks such as ISO 27001. Regardless of the facts and circumstances at play, the process outlines decision-making criteria and responses that apply in all scenarios. Ad hoc approaches to compliance, on the other hand, require a great level of understanding of the facts and circumstances at play in each individual case.

So, although the CPRA only imposes an obligation of "reasonable security," it is not difficult to see how this obligation works in practice. Good, "reasonable" security will likely involve a level of encryption surrounding the data elements outlined in section 81.5. It will also involve a risk-based approach to security management. Applying encryption more widely may also prove beneficial, because the loss of encrypted information poses no problem under the CPRA.

Section 150 includes some extra considerations. Subparagraph (a)(1) states that a consumer's right to pursue civil action applies when personal information "is subject to an unauthorized access and exfiltration, theft, or disclosure." It is important to consider the full range of data-loss scenarios, as each may pose liability to the organization. Data may be stolen, as is often the case with criminal hackers. Data can also be stolen internally – either directly, through employees and personnel (e.g. someone looking to take work product, trade secrets, or client account information to their next employer), or indirectly, through consultants and contracts (e.g. Target's 2014 hack was caused in part by vulnerabilities with the heating, ventilation, and air-conditioning provider). Data can also be inadvertently exposed – sending emails to the wrong person, or accidentally posting files on a public web page. There is no shortage of examples in the media that detail the latest embarrassing data breach. Many of these types of incidents can be controlled and contained through technological solutions (e.g. data loss prevention (DLP) tools). A level of general assurance can also be provided through internal training. Everyone at the organization should be aware of their responsibility for cybersecurity, data privacy, and good data governance. Make sure they understand how their actions, no matter how inadvertent or minor, can subject the whole organization to risk.

Remember that the CPRA really only requires organizations to maintain reasonable security. Ideally, this involves a risk-based approach to information security management and some element of training to ensure all personnel are aware of threats, liabilities, and how to avoid them.

CHAPTER 7: PENALTIES

Interestingly, the consumer enforcement mechanism outlined in section 150 is quite narrow in scope. In particular, consumer enforcement under the CPRA is much narrower than the provisions originally included in Mactaggart's ballot proposal. As mentioned earlier, consumers can only bring a civil action for failure to "implement and maintain reasonable security procedures and practices."[171] Consumer civil suits cannot be based on violations of any other section of the statute.[172] Therefore, at the time of writing, consumers will not be able to bring claims against an organization for, say, failure to respond to a consumer request within the appropriate time frame, or failure to delete data. Consumers may institute civil action against an organization only for loss of non-encrypted and non-redacted information caused by a failure to maintain reasonable security.

The penalties under this provision are relatively small, although they can stack up, especially in a class-action case. Damages are limited to actual damages caused by the data's loss, or statutory damages ranging from $100–750 per consumer, per incident.[173] When determining the amount of statutory damages, courts will consider "any one or more of

---

[171] Cal. Civ. Code § 1798.150(a).

[172] Cal. Civ. Code § 1798.150(c).

[173] Cal. Civ. Code § 1798.150(a)(1)(A).

the relevant circumstances […] including, but not limited to"[174].

- The nature and seriousness of the misconduct
- The number of violations
- The persistence of the misconduct
- The length of time over which the misconduct occurred
- The wilfulness of the defendant's misconduct; and
- The defendant's assets, liabilities, and net worth

Whichever amount is higher – statutory or actual – will be the amount used for damages. So, if a consumer cannot demonstrate actual financial harm caused by the data loss, they will be limited to the statutory cap. Of course, the court may also grant an injunction, or any other relief that it deems proper.[175]

It is quite complicated to enforce the consumer civil suit provision, however. When pursuing a case for statutory damages, a consumer (or class of consumers) must provide 30 days' written notice before initiating an action against an organization.[176] Note that this notice is not required to initiate an action solely for actual damages suffered; the 30-day notice rule only applies to cases pursuing statutory damages.[177]

---

[174] Cal. Civ. Code § 1798.150(a)(2).

[175] Cal. Civ. Code § 1798.150(a)(1)(B),(C).

[176] Cal. Civ. Code § 1798.150(b).

[177] Ibid.

In their notice, the consumer should identify specific provisions of the CPRA that are alleged to have been violated. The organization then has 30 days to cure the violation. Assuming the violation is cured, the organization should provide a written statement to the consumer explaining that the violation has been resolved and that no further violations will occur. Under these conditions, no action for statutory damages may proceed.[178]

If an organization continues to violate the CPRA "in breach of the express written statement provided to the consumer," only then can the consumer initiate an action against the organization. Technically, this action is only to enforce the written statement, and to pursue statutory damages for each breach of the statement.[179]

Remember that consumers can only initiate action against an organization for failure to maintain reasonable security. Conversely, California's attorney general, or the newly created California Privacy Protection Agency, can bring a suit for violation of any part of the statute, e.g. failure to respond to a consumer request within 45 calendar days. Here, penalties for statutory violations are limited to $2,500 per violation, up to $7,500 for each intentional violation.[180] Injunction is also available as a remedy.[181]

---

[178] Cal. Civ. Code § 1798.150(b).

[179] Ibid.

[180] Cal. Civ. Code § 1798.155(a).

[181] Ibid.

CHAPTER 8: BREACH NOTIFICATIONS

California already has rules governing data breaches and breach notification in sections 80–84 of the California Civil Code,[182] which deal with the maintenance of "customer records."

Section 82(a) deals with data breach notifications for a business, and it covers several areas. First, there are requirements that apply to an organization that "owns or licenses computerized data that includes personal information." Any "person or business that conducts business in California" that owns or licenses such information is required to disclose a data security breach to California residents. Here, a "breach" is defined as the unauthorized acquisition of unencrypted personal information. A breach may also include the loss of encrypted information, if the respective encryption key or other security credential was also lost. The important point is whether the organization has "a reasonable belief that the encryption key or security credential could render that (encrypted) personal information readable or useable." Ultimately, the issue is whether the organization lost readily readable or useable information.

If an organization that owns or licenses personal information suffers a breach, it is required to disclose it following either discovery or notification of the breach. Disclosures are to be made to California residents "in the most expedient time possible and without unreasonable delay." What that time

---

[182] Cal. Civ. Code § 1798.82.

frame will actually look like in practice will likely be dictated by evolving case law, because what constitutes an "unreasonable delay" may be different depending on the circumstances of the case concerned. The law does point out that expediency may be dictated by "any measures necessary to determine the scope of the breach and restore the reasonable integrity of the data system." As a result, any forensic analysis, technical investigations, or remediation and clean-up activities may provide a justifiable, "reasonable" delay. However, that does not permit organizations to use these activities as excuses to avoid the inevitable. California residents need to be notified, and in deference to their privacy rights (as the organization lost their data), disclosure should be made as soon as realistically possible.

In practice, this means organizations need to develop an incident response management process that facilitates quick and efficient investigation of issues. Should a security event occur, the organization should be poised to not only respond to the incident itself but also to analyze the privacy impact and, in turn, notify affected consumers. This requires a great deal of coordination among IT or information security functions, the general counsel or legal department, and any marketing or public relations personnel who can help craft the actual disclosure message. Technical employees are required to understand, investigate, and eliminate the breach (while also learning from the issue in order to avoid similar issues in the future); legal is necessary to determine the threshold analysis required for disclosure, and to prepare the organization for any potential litigation or liability; and marketing/PR is needed to help with outreach to customers, business partners, investors, and potentially media outlets, who all may be interested in what is going on.

Ideally, all personnel at an organization should have a general understanding of information security issues and the symptoms of a possible attack or event. This is why awareness training is critical for all staff – everyone in the organization plays a role in managing information security. Of course, certain personnel play much larger roles (e.g. IT/IS). Not all employees need to understand the incident response management process. For example, it is likely unnecessary for front-end sales staff to understand the internal investigation and escalation processes related to information security incidents. Most personnel just need to understand who to contact if they think there is an issue. Dedicated support staff can take it from there, engaging in the necessary investigation and analysis to determine whether the issue rises to the level of an information security event or full-blown data breach. Those staff can contact relevant parties (e.g. legal, PR, senior management, etc.) as necessary.

Slightly different rules apply to organizations that maintain personal information that the business does not own. Those organizations are required to notify the owner or licensee of such information "immediately following discovery."[183] There are no carve-outs for measures to restore the integrity of the system, or questions of what constitutes reasonable vs. unreasonable delay. The notification must be made immediately, as soon as the breach is discovered. This will require close coordination between relevant teams or personnel that manage the incident response process.

---

[183] Cal. Civ. Code § 1798.82(b).

The statute goes on to provide detail related to the actual form and substance of the notification itself. Subparagraph (d) of section 82 outlines certain requirements. The notification must be "written in plain language, [...] titled 'Notice of Data Breach.'" It must also include certain details related to the breach, formatted in certain ways.

At a minimum, the following detail must be included in the breach notification[184]:

- The date that the notice is provided
- The name and contact information of the reporting person or business
- A list of the types of personal information that were or are reasonably believed to have been the subject of a breach
- A general description of the breach incident, if that information is possible to determine at the time the notice is provided
- Any of the following, if it is possible to determine at the time the notice is provided:
  - The date of the breach
  - The estimated date of the breach
  - The date range within which the breach occurred
- Whether notification was delayed as a result of a law enforcement investigation
- The toll-free telephone numbers and addresses of major credit reporting agencies if the breach exposed Social

---

[184] Cal. Civ. Code § 1798.82(d)(2)(A)–(G).

Security numbers, driver's license numbers, or California identification card numbers
- An offer to provide "appropriate identity theft prevention and mitigation services" to affected individuals at no cost for at least 12 months. However, this only applies if:
  o The person or business providing the notification was the source of the breach
  o The breach exposed Social Security numbers, driver's license numbers, or California identification card numbers

This detail must be presented under the following headings[185]:

- "What Happened"
- "What Information Was Involved"
- "What We Are Doing"
- "What You Can Do"
- "For More Information"

There are even formatting requirements. Titles and headings "shall be clearly and conspicuously displayed," the notice must be designed "to call attention to the nature and significance of the information it contains," and the text can be no smaller than ten-point font.[186]

---

[185] Cal. Civ. Code § 1798.82(d)(1).

[186] Cal. Civ. Code § 1798.82(d)(1)(A)–(C).

All of the above apply to written notices, but written notices are not the only method available to organizations. Should an organization choose to use a written notice, the statute helpfully provides a model security breach notification form – see Table 2.

Table 2: Model Security Breach Notification Form

[NAME OF INSTITUTION / LOGO] _____ _____ Date: [insert date]	
NOTICE OF DATA BREACH	
What Happened?	
What Information Was Involved?	

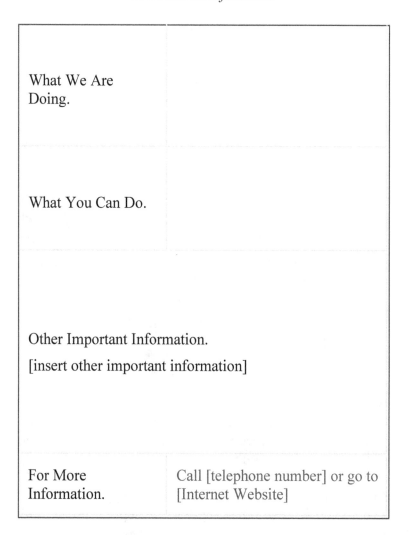

What We Are Doing.	
What You Can Do.	
Other Important Information. [insert other important information]	
For More Information.	Call [telephone number] or go to [Internet Website]

Other methods of notice are available. If the organization can demonstrate that the cost of providing individual notices would exceed $250,000, the number of affected people exceeds 500,000, or sufficient contact information is not available, the organization can rely on "substitute notice."[187] Substitute notice requires all of the following[188]:

- Email notice when the organization has an email address for those affected
- If the organization maintains a web page, there should be "conspicuous posting" of the notice there for at least 30 days.

> "conspicuous posting [...] means providing a link to the notice on the home page or first significant page after entering the Internet Web site that is in larger type than the surrounding text, or in contrasting type, font, or color to the surrounding text of the same size, or set off from the surrounding text of the same size by symbols or other marks that call attention to the link"

- Notification to major state-wide media

In the event of a security breach involving only login credentials (i.e. a username or email address, in combination with a password or security question and answer that would permit access to an online account), the organization may provide notice by directing affected individuals to promptly change their password and related security questions or answers, or to take other appropriate steps to protect any

---

[187] Cal. Civ. Code § 1798.82(j)(3).

[188] Cal. Civ. Code § 1798.82(j)(3)(A)–(C).

online accounts that use the same login credentials.[189] It should be noted that if the breach involves login credentials for an email account provided by the organization, sending a notification to that affected email address does not constitute notice.[190] In such cases, the organization should rely on one of the other notice methods mentioned above (e.g. conspicuous posting on the organization's website).

It is important to note that penalties for violations of those sections of the California Civil Code dealing with the maintenance of "customer records" are separate from the penalties outlined in the CPRA.[191] Any customer may initiate civil action to recover damages caused by violation of this statute.[192] Additional penalties apply to organizations that violate section 1798.83 of the statute, which deals with organizations that share personal information with third parties, knowing those third parties intend to use the information for direct marketing purposes. This is explained in chapter 9.

---

[189] Cal. Civ. Code § 1798.82(j)(4).

[190] Cal. Civ. Code § 1798.82(j)(5).

[191] Cal. Civ. Code § 1798.84.

[192] Cal. Civ. Code § 1798.84(b).

CHAPTER 9: OTHER RELATED LAWS – MAINTAINING CUSTOMER RECORDS

There are rules in California statute that govern the maintenance and disposal of customer records. Although the overlap with those laws is somewhat confusing, they should be noted as they cover many of the same or similar topics.

For example, there are rules that apply to third parties that use personal information for direct marketing, and they are substantially similar to the "right of access" rules. Here, the rules apply to:

- A "business" that has "an established business relationship with a customer"; and ...
- The business disclosed personal information to third parties within the preceding calendar year; and ...
- "the business knows or reasonably should know that the third parties used the personal information for the third parties' direct marketing purposes"

If these apply, then the business must disclose certain information to customers who request this information.[193] It is important to note that these obligations do not apply to "a business with fewer than 20 full-time or part-time employees."[194]

---

[193] Cal. Civ. Code § 1798.83(a).

[194] Cal. Civ. Code § 1798.83(c)(1).

Note that the language here uses "customer" rather than "consumer," which is used in the CPRA. "Customer" is defined as "an individual who provides personal information to a business for the purpose of purchasing or leasing a product or obtaining a service from the business."[195] So, under this provision, a business needs to prepare responses to all customers, not just California residents (i.e. "consumers").

There is a specific definition of "personal information" used with regard to this provision. That is, section 1798.83 does not reference the definition of "personal information" found in relevant portions of the CPRA dealing with "right of access" requests. As a result, organizations that collect personal information will be required to disclose certain things; organizations that sell personal information will be required to disclose certain things; and organizations that give personal information to third parties that in turn use it for marketing will be required to disclose certain things. This may seem like a compliance challenge, but the solution is simple – transparency. The more an organization provides insight into its data processing activities in full detail, the less likely that organization will get tripped up by the various reporting requirements found in California law, and other national and international laws.

For purposes of disclosure under section 1798.83, "personal information" is defined as all of the following categories[196]:

- Name and address

---

[195] Cal. Civ. Code § 1798.80(c).

[196] Cal. Civ. Code § 1798.83(e)(6)(A).

- Electronic mail address
- Age or date of birth
- Names of children
- Electronic mail or other addresses of children
- Number of children
- The age or gender of children
- Height
- Weight
- Race
- Religion
- Occupation
- Telephone number
- Education
- Political party affiliation
- Medical condition
- Drugs, therapies, or medical products or equipment used
- The kind of product the customer purchased, leased, or rented
- Real property purchased, leased, or rented
- The kind of service provided
- Social Security number
- Bank account number
- Credit card number
- Debit card number
- Bank or investment account, debit card, or credit card balance
- Payment history

- Information pertaining to the customer's creditworthiness, assets, income, or liabilities

As can be seen, the categories of personal information provided in section 1798.83 are much more detailed than the categories of personal information provided in the CPRA.

So, if an organization provides personal information to third parties, and those third parties then use it for their own direct marketing purposes, the organization must disclose certain things about that arrangement to its customers. That process requires a few things.

First, information must be provided to customers free of charge.[197] This theme is increasingly common in data privacy laws. The idea is that companies cannot charge customers in an attempt to discourage transparency; people should be able to freely know how their data is used.

Second, the organization must designate either a mailing address, email address, telephone, or fax number where customer requests can be sent.[198] Once this is complete, the organization must then do at least one of the following:

- All agents, managers, and employees "who regularly have contact with customers" must be informed of the contact details so they can provide that information to customers.[199] Affected organizations will need to prepare relevant training materials, and document that

---

[197] Cal. Civ. Code § 1798.83(a).

[198] Cal. Civ. Code § 1798.83(b)(1).

[199] Cal. Civ. Code § 1798.83(b)(1)(A).

such training occurred, in order to effectively demonstrate that it met its obligations to instruct employees.

OR

- Contact details must be "readily available upon request of a customer at every place of business in California where the business or its agents regularly have contact with customers."[200] Ideally, this is already a natural occurrence – organizations should make it easy for consumers to contact them with questions regarding personal information, regardless of where the customer is located (one more reason to design a global, external privacy policy that is readily accessible across an organization's web presence).

OR

- Create web links to its privacy policies. Organizations can do so by either of the following:
  - Add to the home page of its Web site a link to a page titled "Your Privacy Rights"[201]

The first page of the resulting link must provide the contact details for submitting customer requests (i.e. mailing address, email address, telephone or fax number).[202] It must

---

[200] Cal. Civ. Code § 1798.83(b)(1)(C).

[201] Cal. Civ. Code § 1798.83(b)(1)(B).

[202] Cal. Civ. Code § 1798.83(b)(1)(B).

also describe a customer's rights as they apply to this section of law (not the provisions of the CPRA).[203]

OR

- "Add the words 'Your Privacy Rights' to the home page's link to the business's privacy policy."[204]

In this case, the words "Your Privacy Rights" must be in the same style and size as the original link to the privacy policy.[205]

There are other requirements related to formatting the text of the words "Your Privacy Rights" for organizations that do not maintain a privacy policy. This is inadvisable, though. All organizations, regardless of how or where they operate, should prepare and publish a privacy policy or data processing notice. This is not only a sensible business strategy in today's economy but also an explicit requirement of many other state and sector-specific privacy laws that likely also apply to the organization.

Regardless of how the customer makes their request, the organization must reply in either writing or email.[206] The response must include a listing of all the categories outlined above that were disclosed "for the third parties' direct marketing purposes during the immediately preceding

---

[203] Cal. Civ. Code § 1798.83(b)(1)(B).

[204] Ibid.

[205] Ibid.

[206] Cal. Civ. Code § 1798.83(a)(1),(2).

calendar year."[207] It must also include the names and addresses of all third parties that received personal information for their direct marketing purposes in the preceding calendar year.[208] However, organizations are only obligated to reply to a customer "once during the course of any calendar year."[209] In addition, organizations are not obligated "to provide information associated with specific individuals and may provide the information required by this section in standardized format."[210]

Responses must be provided within 30 days (not the 45 granted by the CPRA).[211] If the organization receives a request for information outside of one of its dedicated channels, the organization must provide a response "within a reasonable period [...] but not to exceed 150 days from the date received."[212] Nevertheless, organizations would be well advised to align themselves against a single, limited time frame for responding to all consumer requests for information, rather than trying to manage requests separately according to different communication channels, and thus different time frame requirements. It will likely be much easier to use one standard across the entire organization.

---

[207] Cal. Civ. Code § 1798.83(a)(1).

[208] Cal. Civ. Code § 1798.83(a)(2).

[209] Cal. Civ. Code § 1798.83(c)(1).

[210] Cal. Civ. Code § 1798.83(b)(3).

[211] Cal. Civ. Code § 1798.83(b)(1)(C).

[212] Cal. Civ. Code § 1798.83(b)(1)(C).

Part of the consumer response process should also involve follow-up communications, as consumers are likely to ask clarifying questions or request additional information. Personnel responsible for responding to consumers should be educated on proper response protocols. Communications should also be documented to track what was said and when. This is not only important in demonstrating compliance but also in defending against legal claims. If an organization is alleged to have violated a provision of section 1798.83, it may be able to defend itself against those claims by providing evidence that it did respond to the consumer request properly, with complete and accurate information, within a certain time frame.[213] The Attorney General's Regulations also indicate that organizations should maintain records of consumer requests for at least 24 months.[214]

Some organizations that share personal information with third parties for direct marketing purposes may already offer a way for their customers to either agree to, or opt-out of, such sharing. If an organization does offer a way for customers to exercise choice around sharing data with third parties, the organization can comply with the disclosure requirements set out in section 1798.83(a) by simply notifying the customer of their right to prevent disclosure, and providing a cost-free means to exercise that right.[215]

Failure to meet the disclosure requirements of section 1798.83 can subject a company to civil actions initiated by

---

[213] Cal. Civ. Code § 1798.84(d).

[214] AG Regulations §999.317(b), (c).

[215] Cal. Civ. Code § 1798.83(c)(2).

customers.[216] Civil penalties are currently limited to $500 per violation, or up to $3,000 for willful, reckless, or intentional violations.[217] These fines are cumulative, though, and can be imposed on an organization in addition to fines imposed for violations of CPRA statutes.[218] Prevailing plaintiffs are also entitled to recover "reasonable attorney's fees and costs," which can increase the total cost of litigation for a liable organization.[219] It may also encourage a certain degree of vexatious litigation against organizations, in the hope that an organization will settle any claims before potentially proceeding to court (and in turn, increasing the amount of attorney's fees that the organization may have to pay for). As a result, organizations should take special care to comply with section 1798.83 disclosure requirements, in addition to the disclosure requirements in the CPRA.

California businesses are also required to take reasonable steps to dispose of customer records in a way that makes them unreadable or undecipherable.[220] In addition, businesses are required to "implement and maintain reasonable security procedures and practices appropriate to the nature of the information, to protect [it] from unauthorized access, destruction, use, modification, or

---

[216] Cal. Civ. Code § 1798.84(b).

[217] Cal. Civ. Code § 1798.84(c).

[218] Cal. Civ. Code § 1798.84(h).

[219] Cal. Civ. Code § 1798.84(g).

[220] Cal. Civ. Code § 1798.81.

disclosure," similar to Article 30 of the GDPR and various other US state data breach laws.[221]

---

[221] Cal. Civ. Code § 1798.81.5(b),(c).

CHAPTER 10: THE CPRA

The text as of December, 2020

Presently, the CCPA has not been updated on the California Legislative Information website to reflect the CCPA's transition into the CPRA.

For now, you can access the official text of the CPRA here:

www.oag.ca.gov/system/files/initiatives/pdfs/19-0021A1%20%28Consumer%20Privacy%20-%20Version%203%29_1.pdf.

However, note that there may be legislative measures in the meantime that will amend the text of the CPRA and will not be reflected in the document above.

In the near future, the CPRA will be added to the California Legislative Information website, and you will be able to access the Regulation here:

https://leginfo.legislature.ca.gov/faces/home.xhtml.

FURTHER READING

IT Governance Publishing (ITGP) is the world's leading publisher for governance and compliance. Our industry-leading pocket guides, books, training resources, and toolkits are written by real-world practitioners and thought leaders. They are used globally by audiences of all levels, from students to C-suite executives.

Our high-quality publications cover all IT governance, risk, and compliance frameworks, and are available in a range of formats. This ensures our customers can access the information they need in the way they need it.

Other resources you may find useful include:

- *ISO/IEC 27701:2019 – An introduction to privacy information management* by Steve Watkins and Alan Shipman, *www.itgovernancepublishing.co.uk/product/iso-iec-27701-2019-an-introduction-to-privacy-information-management*
- *EU General Data Protection Regulation (GDPR) – An implementation and compliance guide, fourth edition* by the IT Governance Privacy Team, *www.itgovernancepublishing.co.uk/product/eu-general-data-protection-regulation-gdpr-an-implementation-and-compliance-guide-fourth-edition*
- *CPRA Compliance Gap Assessment Tool* by IT Governance Publishing,

www.itgovernancepublishing.co.uk/product/cpra-compliance-gap-assessment-tool

For more information on ITGP and branded publishing services, and to view our full list of publications, visit *www.itgovernancepublishing.co.uk*.

To receive regular updates from ITGP, including information on new publications in your area(s) of interest, sign up for our newsletter at *www.itgovernancepublishing.co.uk/topic/newsletter*.

Branded publishing

Through our branded publishing service, you can customize ITGP publications with your organization's branding.

Find out more at *www.itgovernancepublishing.co.uk/topic/branded-publishing-services*.

Related services

ITGP is part of GRC International Group, which offers a comprehensive range of complementary products and services to help organizations meet their objectives.

For a full range of resources on data privacy solutions visit *www.itgovernanceusa.com/data-privacy-solutions*

Training services

The IT Governance training program is built on our extensive practical experience designing and implementing management systems based on ISO standards, best practice, and regulations.

Our courses help attendees develop practical skills and comply with contractual and regulatory requirements. They also support career development via recognized qualifications.

Learn more about our training courses in data protection and view the full course catalog at *www.itgovernanceusa.com/training*.

Professional services and consultancy

We are a leading global consultancy of IT governance, risk management, and compliance solutions. We advise organizations around the world on their most critical issues, and present cost-saving and risk-reducing solutions based on international best practice and frameworks.

We offer a wide range of delivery methods to suit all budgets, timescales, and preferred project approaches.

Find out how our consultancy services can help your organization at *www.itgovernanceusa.com/consulting*.

Industry news

Want to stay up to date with the latest developments and resources in the IT governance and compliance market? Subscribe to our Weekly Round-up newsletter and we will send you mobile-friendly emails with fresh news and features about your preferred areas of interest, as well as unmissable offers and free resources to help you successfully start your projects. *www.itgovernanceusa.com/weekly-round-up*.